Coach Mike Garland has ma ▮▮▮▮▮▮
program and all the former playe.. ....., ...
together and in all his years there because of his passion, enthusiasm, and knowledge
of basketball. More importantly, he truly cared for the student athletes and how he
engaged with us to make us the best versions of ourselves every single day. I would
recommend his book to any individual, business, or organization that is interested in
developing a culture of High Performance Maximum Xecution.

—**Mat Ishbia**, *Founder and CEO of United Wholesale Mortgages, Owner of the Phoenix Suns*

* * *

I gravitated to Coach G the first moment I stepped on campus. He had a unique ability
to connect with all the players on our team. I appreciated him because I know he cared
about me and had my best interest at heart. We spent a lot of time together because
we both had a passion for winning. I learned a lot from Coach G, not only basketball
related things but leadership and life skills as well. He played a major role in helping us
win a national championship!! He definitely had a huge impact on my life!!

—**Mateen Cleaves**, *Former MSU 2000 National Champion All American, Leader of Executive Leadership at United Wholesale Mortgages*

* * *

Honestly, accountability, toughness, and leading with love are the pillars of Michigan
State Basketball. There is no better person to exemplify these qualities than Coach G.
Michigan State Basketball is not the great powerhouse without Mike Garland. Every
student athlete that had the privilege to get to know Coach G knew life was bigger than
basketball. He cared about the person you were becoming more than the basketball
player. That's tough to say for coaches because their livelihood is based on wins and
losses. Coach Garland knew the secret to get the most out of everyone. He knew to
show genuine care about players' wellbeing off the court, and they would run through
a wall for him. I would recommend this book to any individual, business, or organization
that is seriously interested in developing a culture of winning and High Performance
Maximum Xecution.

—**Travis Walton**, *Former MSU Basketball Team Captain (3 years), World Renown Basketball Skill Trainer*

For each book sold, a donation will be made
to the Champions of the Heart Foundation.

AGOGE

The Spartan School of
High Performance
Maximum Xecution Training
A Playbook of Life Lessons

Michael "OG" Garland

AGOGE
The Spartan School of
High Performance Maximum Xecution Training

Copyright © 2023 by "OG" Michael Garland

Learn more at

maximumXecution.com

This book is a tribute to my cherished wife, Cynthia, and our three children, Quentin, Simone, and Michael Ray, as well as my eight beloved grandchildren. It is also dedicated to every individual who has left a mark on my life, and to all those whom I have had the honor of coaching, teaching, or mentoring throughout my career. To each of you, it has never been solely about what I have provided, but rather about the invaluable inspiration and knowledge that you have imparted to me, and continue to offer to others. I hold deep affection for all of you!

OG

THE PLAYBOOK

OGOGE PRE-GAME SPEECH Prologue ix

INTRODUCTION x

CHAPTER ONE Characteristic #1 – Possessing the 7 Fundamentals
Cassius Winston...1

Fundamental #1 Passing **Mama Seed & Tom Izzo** 12

Fundamental #2 Dribbling **Mateen Cleaves**.....................................26

Fundamental #3 Shooting **Morris (Mo Pete) Peterson** 40

Fundamental #4 Rebounding **Adreian (AP) Payne Tom (Chief) Izzo** ..60

Fundamental #5 Playing with Speed and Quickness **Steve Smith**........73

Fundamental #6 Toughness **Andre (Dre) Hutson Michael (Ray) Garland**... 79

Fundamental #7 – Playing with Intelligence **"Intelligence with toughness is lethal" Tom Izzo** 88

CHAPTER TWO Characteristic #2 – Talent "Talent Is Never Enough"
Branden BJ Dawson... 98

INTANGIBLE WINNING TRAIT ONE TALENT HAS TO WORK HARD
(BE A HARD WORKER) **Denzel Valentine** 106

INTANGIBLE WINNING TRAIT TWO TALENT HAS TO BE SELF
MOTIVATED AND DISCIPLINE **Bryn Forbes** 111

INTANGIBLE WINNING TRAIT THREE TALENT HAS TO HAVE
PASSION **Tom Izzo, Draymond Green and Magic Johnson**..........116

INTANGIBLE WINNING TRAIT FOUR TALENT HAS TO HAVE
INTENSITY,ENERGY & ENTHUSIASM **LouRawls (Tum Tum) Narin Jr**
....119

INTANGIBLE WINNING TRAIT FIVE TALENT HAS TO BE CONFIDENT
AND HAVE COMPETITIVE DRIVE **Miles Bridges**............................124

INTANGIBLE WINNING TRAIT SIX TALENT HAS TO HAVE GOOD
LEADERSHIP "Leadership Has To Be Willing To Confront and Demand"
Draymond (DayDay) Green & Travis Walton 129

INTANGIBLE WINNING TRAIT SEVEN TALENT HAS TO HAVE
G.U.T.S, **Quentin, Simone & Michael Ray Garland** 136

CHAPTER THREE Characteristic #3 – Coachable **Mike (OG) Garland
Draymond (DayDay) Green**..144

CHAPTER FOUR Characteristic #4 – Self Discipline Deep Practice ...148

CHAPTER FIVE Characteristic #5 – The Gamer "Be at your Best when your Best is needed" **Travis Trice** 154

CHAPTER SIX Characteristic #6 – Resilience "The Antidote for Adversity" Playing Through Fatigue and Adversity **Tom Izzo**...................................... 166

CHAPTER SEVEN Characteristic #7 – The Playmaker "Can you make other (people) players better" **Draymond Green, Tom Izzo, Earvin (Magic) Johnson** 170

BONUS CHAPTERS 183

GREAT PLAYERS HAVE A GREAT FIRST STEP **Alan Anderson** ... 183

PLAYING GREAT DEFENSE GUARDS AGAINST UPSETS **Gary Harris** 188

CHIEF **Tom Izzo**... 191

OG **Mike Garland**... 200

POST GAME SPEECH Epilogue.. 206

ABOUT THE AUTHOR... 208

OGOGE

PRE-GAME SPEECH

Prologue

In my book Agoge, I capture the essence of Tom Izzo's Spartan school of basketball training as it pertains to preparing players to be high-performance, maximum execution players (people) in the game of life. Ironically, the Spartan basketball program resembles the ancient Greek Spartan Agoge school of rigorous training and education mandated for all ancient Greek Spartan males. Consequently, my book reveals to the reader how lessons learned through basketball can be used to become successful high-performance, maximum execution participants in the game of life. It is believed by experts in the game of basketball that more games are lost than won. Without question, this quote also holds true for the game of life as well.

An in-depth examination of the game of basketball can remarkably reveal little-known secrets that pertain to simple fundamental concepts in basketball. These concepts translate into high-performance, maximum execution, and winning strategies in life. My book contains analogies that provide a clear picture of these game-winning fundamental concepts, which have been hidden secrets within the game of basketball. Agoge unlocks the door to these secrets, guiding you through these simple yet complex concepts that are unimaginable to conventional thinking processes regarding success in both basketball and life. The little-known secrets revealed in this book were derived from an accumulation of pertinent information and experiences gathered over the course of a passionate lifetime coaching career in basketball.

INTRODUCTION

"Our 2019 victory over Duke came down to a single, solitary moment in time. In retrospect, this moment was the time between the basketball leaving Kenny Goins' hands and the crowd roaring as the ball passed through the net. The end result of these frozen moments of silence is often minuscule, life-changing occasions that usually end one of two ways: the joy of victory or the agony of defeat. Both scenarios are contingent on the ability of players to successfully execute at a high-performance, maximum execution level when needed. The same high-performance, maximum execution is no different if you want to be successful in the game of life. However, you must be properly prepared if you want to execute your own personal game plan for life. If you're not, you will consistently taste the agony of defeat throughout your entire life.

I decided to write this book to give readers an in-depth and comprehensive description of how the seven characteristics commonly found among all successful basketball players (people) can significantly improve your chances for success in the game of life. On the night of our Duke game, fortunately for us, our team executed our game plan at a high-performance, maximum execution level. Kenny Goins's game-winning shot was the result of a play we had repetitively practiced throughout the season. As a matter of fact, the shot was not intended for Kenny; he was actually the third option in the play. His job was to pass the ball to Cassius Winston first and Xavier Tillman second. In hindsight, his decision to take the shot was the best because he was the player who was open due to the way Duke decided to guard the play.

That night, Kenny was not only prepared to make the shot, but more importantly, he was prepared to make the right decision, which was to take the shot. He had been repetitiously trained over the course of his career to trust the seven common characteristics of success found throughout the pages of this book. Oprah Winfrey, the billionaire talk show host and entrepreneur, ends all of her interviews with a question I love. Her last question is always, "WHAT DO YOU KNOW FOR SURE?" The first time I heard it, I had to ask myself, "What do I know for sure?" Well, what I know for sure is that basketball is merely a microcosm of the game of life. Once you've carefully examined my seven characteristics common to all successful teams and players, you will begin to think of the game of basketball from a totally different perspective. A perspective that you probably would never have imagined as a legitimate thought process; a perspective that depicts how the fundamental concepts of a simple game, when properly adopted, can positively impact every aspect of your life. The seven characteristics outlined in this book were derived from 41 years of coaching high school and college basketball. I've spent most of those years, 23 to be exact, as an assistant for my trusted friend, coaching mentor, and college teammate, Hall of Fame coach "Chief" Tom Izzo. The vast majority of the basketball world is well aware of our numerous accomplishments over the course of our careers, the most notable being our 2000 National Championship, eight Final Four appearances, eight BIG 10 championships, and 19 NBA players.

However, what has been most meaningful to both Chief (Tom Izzo) and myself are the success stories of our former players who did not play in the NBA, as well as the student managers and student secretaries who have become successful individuals in their own right. Additionally, we have been able to graduate 85% of our players. If asked, I don't think, I know that Chief (Tom Izzo) would agree that our ability to successfully influence the quality of life and career paths of these young men and women is the direct result of using basketball analogies to teach them valuable life lessons that enhance their opportunities to become high-performance, maximum execution players in the game of life. Now, let's throw the ball up and get the game started!

CHAPTER ONE

Characteristic #1 – Possessing the 7 Fundamentals

Cassius Winston

Cassius Winston has unequivocally mastered the seven basic fundamental skills required to play basketball proficiently. Despite not possessing the elite athleticism or physical superiority commonly found in most superstars, he possesses an uncanny ability to instantaneously alter the outcome of a game. Throughout both the 2019 and 2020 seasons, he arguably changed the outcomes of more games than any other player in college basketball. His intelligence, court awareness, and skillful proficiency of the seven fundamentals are the three common denominators that drive his elite high-performance maximum execution level of play. During our 2019 tournament game against Duke, he convincingly demonstrated the proficiency with which he has mastered the fundamental skill set needed to perform at a high-performance maximum execution elite level on college basketball's biggest stage. In that game, he brought us back from an 11-point deficit to an eventual 68-67 victory over Duke, moving us on to the 2019 Final Four.

His high-performance maximum execution play against Duke is clearly a testament to his extraordinary level of mental toughness. After finishing the 2019 season with accolades that recognized him as one of college basketball's elite returning players heading into the upcoming 2020 season, unfortunately, Cassius would begin the 2020 season facing an unspeakable tragedy that burdened him with heartbreak, pain, and sorrow throughout the entire 2019-2020 season. The impetus of his burden came about when his brother Zach took his own life on November 9th, 2019. It is believed that this unforeseen tragedy happened approximately around 9:30 to 10:00 p.m. the night before our game against Binghamton.

Customarily, we meet with the team the night before each home game to watch film and go over the scouting report at 8 o'clock in our film room at the Breslin Center. After the meeting, I normally give our players about half an hour to check into the Kellogg Center, the on-campus hotel where we stay the night before our home games.

Once the team gets settled into the hotel, I instruct one of the captains to inform the rest of the team about the scheduled meeting in my room. During these meetings, I typically share a story that conveys a valuable life lesson relevant to winning the game the following night. Often, I recount a humorous anecdote involving myself, a family member, or a childhood friend from Willow Run, Michigan. Before concluding the meeting, I inform the players of the designated time for bed check in their respective rooms. However, on this particular night, I went to Cassius's room for the check-in and found him absent. Occasionally, it's not uncommon for one of the guys to be in another teammate's room, engaging in conversation, laughter, and camaraderie.

But on this particular night, after completing my checks, Cassius wasn't in anyone else's room and nowhere to be found. At the time, I still didn't think much of it because our guys would order food and wait in the lobby to pick it up, and they always returned to their rooms once it was delivered. However, when I went back to his room, after giving him what I thought was ample time to get back, he still wasn't there. I then asked his roommate, Foster Loyer, where he was, and he said he really didn't know but thought that he might be down in the lobby talking to his girlfriend, Erin. I called his cell phone and got no answer. After that, I immediately sent him a text message but still received no response.

At that point, I was pissed and wondering what kind of BS he was trying to pull. Yet, at the same time, I felt that something might be wrong but couldn't figure out exactly what it could be because Cassius missing when he knew that he should be in his room was totally out of character for him. Then I went down to the lobby, and he wasn't there either. When I went back up to our floor, I again went to his room and asked Foster to try and reach him on his phone to see if he would answer. However, Foster got no answer either, which again was unusual because, for the most part, even if a player is up to BS, they will usually still pick up the phone for a teammate. Then I was partly pissed and, at the same time, worried because Cassius, throughout his entire career, had never done anything like this before. At that point, I went back to my room to wait for him to come back.

Whenever I'm in the hotel with the team, whether it's at home or on the road, there are a couple of things I do routinely. Firstly, I obtain a key that gives me access to every players' room at any time during the night. I also inform them that I may return after my initial bed check to recheck them throughout the night. Secondly, I keep my room door open until I perceive a decrease in foot traffic on our floor, sometimes leaving it open until 2 or 3 in the morning. I do this for two reasons: first, to be able to hear doors being opened and closed, and second, to observe the movements of our players or anyone else on our floor. I'm primarily more concerned about hotel guests and overly enthusiastic fans, particularly female ones, than I am our players. That's why I always request the room closest to the elevators.

That night, when Cassius finally returned to our floor, I immediately confronted him as he walked past my room, heading towards his own. Remember, I was furious, so I yelled at him, "Hey, dude, where—" Before I could utter the next word, he tearfully blurted out, falling into my arms, drowning in tears and broken down by grief. He said to me "OG, my brother died; he killed himself." We both stood there, embracing each other, in a moment I will never forget. It lasted for about two or three minutes, but honestly, I can't recall the exact duration. What I do remember is the lifelessness I felt throughout his entire body. After briefly composing himself, he said to me, "I need to go be with my teammates." He attempted to walk away, but I continued to embrace him and led him into my room, where I sat him down in a chair.

I then told him that I would go get the guys and bring them to my room. I quickly went to about half of the guys' rooms and told them to bring the remaining guys to my room, while briefly explaining to them what had happened to Cassius's brother, Zach. I recall that many of the guys were asleep because it was nearly midnight. Once everybody arrived in my room, Cassius sorrowfully blurted out again, "My brother killed himself." After that, there wasn't a dry eye amongst us, and the room fell completely silent for at least another 15 minutes. I remember feeling as though time was standing still, as those 15 minutes felt like an hour. As we sat there without uttering a word, the silence was so intense that it seemed as though you could not only see but also feel the body language of every guy, expressing their deepest empathy for Cassius and his brother without actually saying a word.

The news about Zach was very hurtful to our guys because he was frequently on our campus throughout the year. They all knew him and spent a significant amount of time with him, either working out in our gym, hanging out around campus, or just enjoying each other's company in our guys' apartments. Our guys were also friendly with Cassius's younger brother, Khy, as they both played basketball at Albion College, which is only an hour's drive from Lansing. The loving relationship between the three brothers was unlike any other I've seen in my entire life. They were so close that for the most part, wherever you saw one, you would see the other two as well. As we all sat there motionless, Cassius's phone suddenly rang; it was Erin, his girlfriend, letting him know that his parents, Wendy and Reggie, were on their way to the hotel from their home in Detroit, Michigan.

4

A few minutes after the call, Cassius decided to go downstairs to the lobby and wait for his parents. Before he left, I told him that I would walk him downstairs so that I could spend some more time with him. But the real truth was, I didn't want to leave him alone even for a second. However, before Cassius and I left to go downstairs, I told the team to wait in my room until I got back because I wanted to talk to them before they went back to their rooms for the night. After walking Cassius downstairs and handing him off to his girlfriend, I went back upstairs to talk to the guys about what happened and explain to them how quickly a tragedy like this, in just the twinkling of an eye, could change your life forever. Other than that, I don't remember much of anything else I said that night, but I do remember what was said by Josh Langford and Marcus Bingham. Josh spoke up first and said to the guys, "Life is no joke, and we all need to get right with God because not even the next minute is promised to any of us." The room then went into a deeper silence after Josh spoke. Then to my surprise Marcus Bingham spoke up. I would have never guessed that Marcus Bingham, of all our guys, would be the one to speak up so passionately in such grim circumstances. In that moment, Marcus was remarkable. In his two years with us, I had never heard him speak with such passion before. His words weren't profound, but because he spoke from his heart, you could feel the passion in his voice with every word he said. Wisely, he urged every guy to call his parents and tell them exactly what happened to Zach. He said it wouldn't be right for them to hear it from the media before hearing it from all of us first.

Then he animatedly encouraged all of them to tell their parents how much they loved them because, after tonight, for sure you should have learned one thing if nothing else; tomorrow is not promised to you or your parents. After that, the players returned to their rooms, and I went back downstairs to sit with the Winstons. When I got down there, Tom had already arrived and was sitting on the floor, talking to Cassius and his girlfriend.

However, Wendy and Reggie, his parents, weren't there yet, but his younger brother Khy had just arrived with his coach, so I sat on the floor next to Tom and Cassius, talking to Khy and his coach until Wendy and Reggie arrived. A life lesson I learned many years ago is that the best thing you can do for a grieving person is to give them your time, a shoulder to cry on, and the willingness to listen to them. I also learned not to give advice and never to say, "I know how you feel," even if you have gone through a similar situation. How you felt at that time and how the other person feels could be miles apart because everyone handles grief differently.

Once Wendy and Reggie arrived, the entire family, including Erin, embraced each other in a group hug before sitting back down with Tom and myself. I don't know why, but we all sat on the windowsill to the right side of the hotel's entrance door. As we sat there, I could immediately sense an expression of guilt in the body language of both Wendy and Reggie. Eventually, that body language manifested into a serious conversation about what happened to Zach. By the time we were done talking with the Winstons, I decided to go back upstairs to check on the guys. Although it was late, around 5:00 AM to be exact, no one was sleeping because they had been up all night talking about what happened to Zach.

The next morning, I was concerned that our guys would struggle to play well because they hadn't slept a wink all night. When I went to wake them up, to my surprise, every one of them who needed to be woken up had already gotten up and gone to class by the time I reached their rooms. Typically, after ensuring that the players who needed to be up and gone to class were awake, I would usually go home. However, this time I went to the office because I knew that Tom would want to discuss what we could do to help Cassius and his family through their tragedy. When I arrived at the office, we immediately discussed the best way to handle Cassius both in the present and for the rest of the season.

6

By the end of our conversation, we both agreed that he would require assistance which neither of us could provide. Consequently, we called our trainer, Nick Richey, and asked him to contact Lonnie Rosen, our team psychologist. Once we got him on the phone, we explained to him what happened to Cassius's brother, and he suggested what we could do to help Cassius momentarily. A few minutes later, Dr. Rosen, who, by the way, is one of the best sports psychologists in the country, explained to us right away that there are basically three levels of grief associated with survivors of suicide victims: 1) inconsolable grief, 2) guilt, and 3) anger. He said that each one would occur at some point, in no particular order, and that there was no way of knowing how long it would take for Cassius to get through each because it's different for each person. He then suggested that we have Cassius meet with him as soon as possible.

After talking with Lonnie, I told Tom that Tony Dungy should be another person we reach out to for help because he lost his son to suicide. I've known Tony for quite some time, long before he became an NFL Hall of Fame football coach. I first met him through my best friend, Keith Simons, who at the time was playing college football at the university of Minnesota. He had brought Tony to my parents' house to hang out with us as part of his effort to convince him to come play football at the University of Minnesota. The coaching staff asked Keith to help them recruit Tony because he was from Jackson, Michigan, about 45 minutes from my parents' house.

Initially when I called Tony, I didn't reach him, but I knew he would soon call me back and be willing to help us in any way he could. He's a great guy who is a devoted Christian and is all about helping people. When I couldn't reach Tony, Tom and I decided to continue our conversation about what we could do further to help Cassius and his family deal with their ordeal. But before we had a chance to make any progress with our conversation, Tony returned my call. Just as I thought, Tony immediately offered to help. He started talking about the act of suicide, but as he was speaking, I stopped him and told him that Tom was in the room and would like to hear what he was saying. He agreed and then continued to explain to us that the family's issue with guilt is usually the first thing that haunts them because they believe that there was something they could have done to stop Zach from committing suicide. He then said, "But in reality, there is nothing they could have done." Maybe if they happened to be right there when he was making the attempt, they might have been able to physically stop him momentarily. But unfortunately, once a suicidal person has made up their mind to carry out the act, they're going to continue trying until they're finally successful. As for Cassius, he said it would be best for him that we continue to coach him no differently than the way we've coached him throughout his career. Otherwise, we would hamper his healing process. However, as the conversation continued, it was very apparent that Cassius wasn't his biggest worry. Rather, he was more concerned about his mother, Wendy. He felt that Cassius, from the little he knew about him, was mentally tough enough to heal appropriately from what he saw in him while watching him play. However, without even really knowing Wendy, it turned out that his assumption was absolutely right. He based his assumption on what he had gone through with his own wife when their son took his life.

Over the next couple of days, Tony's prediction of how Wendy would handle the guilt associated with Zach's death began to play itself out. The evidence of his prediction became true when she wouldn't leave her hotel room. She was so grief-stricken that she couldn't eat or get out of bed for days.

Our phone call with Tony turned out to be very helpful, especially in terms of coaching Cassius and having an idea of what to expect. Just as we were about to finish the call, Tony said that he would be willing to talk to both Cassius and Wendy whenever they were ready. Tom decided to call Cassius right after we hung up the phone with Tony. He told Cassius that he didn't expect him to play that night and to take as much time as he needed to come back and play. Tom also mentioned that he understood if Cassius decided not to play for the rest of the season. After Tom finished talking to Cassius, he hung up, and we both looked at each other and almost simultaneously said, "I don't know when he's going to play again, or if he will play for the rest of the season."

This particular situation, although not as severe as dealing with a suicide, is a classic example of what it's truly like to be a college basketball coach on a daily basis. Without question, if you win, it's a good job, and you'll get paid well and enjoy all the perks associated with being a successful college basketball coach. However along with that, there is a BIG price to pay in terms of having a shorter life expectancy, no time for a quality family life, and tons of stress from the pressure on you to win. If you do manage to win, then you're expected to maintain an unrealistic level of winning that turns your life into a continuous uphill battle on a slippery slope. What most people don't realize is that on a daily basis, the job of a head college basketball coach is only about 20% coaching the game. The rest of the time, you spend your day putting out fires and dealing with issues. Maybe not to the degree of Cassius's brother committing suicide, but there are usually issues daily. The reason I mention this is to give you a quick mental snapshot of what a day in the life of Tom Izzo looks like, regardless of a tragedy.

Even though we started around 8 AM, we were still a long way from securing the Cassius situation. However, we were forced to change gears because it was nearly 2:00, and it was time for us to head down to the basketball court for our shootaround. As Chief and I walked down to the court, we discussed how we would handle our players during the shootaround. We both agreed that the best thing we could do was simply get through it due to the fragile mental state of our players. As you can imagine, the mood of our entire team and staff was somber at best. The hurt for

Cassius and his family weighed heavily on the hearts and minds of every individual on the court that day as we worked our way through the shoot-around and walk-through.

I'm sure, as you can imagine, the mood of our entire team and staff was somber at best. You could see the hurt for Cassius and his family loom heavy on the hearts and minds of every player and coach that day by their body language as we worked our way through the shootaround. Following the walk-through, we always go right upstairs to our recruiting lounge for our pregame meal. The mood was still the same throughout the meal but even worse because we were all just sitting there eating without anything else to do other than chew our food to occupy our minds. Tom always addresses the team right before everyone is done eating, and that day was no different. He told the team that every guy would have to step up their game because he was 99% sure that Cassius was not going to play.

On game days, our players have to be at the arena an hour and a half before the game, and on the floor 75 minutes before the start of the game for our pregame warm-up. None of us thought that Cassius would play, but we thought that maybe he would show up to support his teammates. However, after about 10 minutes into the warm-up, I saw him jogging through the tunnel, headed for the locker room. Although we all saw him, no one thought he would come out dressed to play in the game, but to everyone's surprise, 5 minutes later, he came to the floor fully dressed for the game.

Once Chief had given the pregame talk and team prayer, we huddled up, and after breaking the huddle, everyone was in tears as we all went to the floor for the start of the game. Of course at the start of the game when they announced Cassius's name, the crowd gave him a standing ovation, which raised the level of emotion even higher. That night, once the game started, Cassius struggled badly, so badly that Tom had to take him out of the game. When he came out of the game, he sat right next to me. I asked him if he was alright, and his response was, "OG, right now it feels like I'm out of my body; I can't even feel the ball.

In the game of basketball, it's very hard to win if your point guard is playing poorly. It doesn't matter who you're playing against, and as a result of Cassius struggling, we found ourselves in a tough game with Binghamton at halftime. Under normal circumstances, Tom and our staff would have been livid, but we knew we couldn't get into players, especially Cassius. However, Tom did say to the team that normally Cassius would have carried them, but tonight it was their turn to carry him. When we came out for the second half, everyone except Cassius was on the floor warming up. Instead, he sat quietly on the bench by himself. As I observed him, it was clear that he wasn't even present in the gym at that moment. When the horn sounded to start the second half, I asked him if he was done for the night. He replied, "No, coach, I need to play."

As the game resumed, we struggled throughout the first five minutes of the second half, and Binghamton started gaining the confidence they needed to beat us. However, something remarkable happened after the 16-minute TV timeout. Cassius instinctively took control of the game, performing as though nothing had ever happened. That night because of his game winning performance we beat Binghamton by 53 points (100-47). Cassius, despite his heartbreak and grief, managed to finish the game with 17 points and 11 assists.

This tragedy teaches us a powerful lesson about the importance of being prepared. It shows us how Cassius's character, determination, and ability to perform at a high level were tested in the face of overwhelming circumstances, such as the recent death of his brother. Despite his heartbreak and grief, Cassius was able to perform exceptionally well. This tragedy highlights the extensive time, hard work, and effort he devoted to mastering the seven fundamental principles that successful people in basketball and in life generally share. His three SUPERPOWERS would have been rendered useless had he not mastered the 7 basic fundamentals of the game before being cast into a situation that should have stripped him of any chance of performing successfully that night. It's not guaranteed that every person taught the 7 fundamentals of basketball will achieve the same level of success on the basketball court as Cassius Winston. However, I do believe that if a person can translate the 7 basic fundamentals of basketball into 7 basic fundamental life skills, then those skills become a significant game changer in terms of their success in life.

Often, players struggle to effectively connect the two different, yet similar aspects of the game of basketball as they pertain to success in the game of basketball and real-life success once their playing days are over. Most of them find it challenging to translate the similarities and differences between these two aspects into practical lessons that apply to their lives.

Throughout the remainder of my book, I will continually set out to prove to you that the analogies I've drawn from the following seven basic fundamentals of basketball—passing, dribbling, shooting, rebounding, playing with speed and quickness, toughness, and intelligence—can be essential factors for success in the game of life.

Fundamental #1 Passing

Mama Seed & Tom Izzo

Wisdom doesn't have to be sophisticated, complex, or hard to understand. In fact, it can easily be taught by using something as simple as passing a basketball to explain how a pass made in the game of basketball can be uniquely similar to a pass made in the game of life. The ability to accurately pass the ball to the right player, at the right time, and in the right place, is, in my opinion, one of the most valuable yet underappreciated skills in the game of basketball.

When a player *passes* the ball to another player and the second player scores a basket, the player that made the *pass* is given what is called an assist and is credited on the game's statistic sheet for making a *pass* that lead to another player scoring a basket. The reason he is credited with an assist is because the player that actually scored the basket, was only able to do so because of the other player that *passed* him the ball. Try to think of it this way: in the context of the game of life, the *Passer* assisted his teammate's efforts to successfully score the basket. A simpler explanation in regards to the game of life, would be the player (person) who made the pass played a significant role in helping someone else succeed.

On a personal level I actually can relate to this analogy because I was fortunate enough to have two great influencers (passers) in my life whose guidance significantly impacted my career path. First and foremost was my grandmother, Bessie Seed, and the other was my college teammate, coaching mentor, and friend, Chief (Tom Izzo). Both of them have remarkable life stories of their own. My grandmother, a devout Christian, survived cancer for 53 years before passing away at the age of 93. On multiple occasions, she told me that she believed God spared her life because she needed to be here to support my mother in raising me, my four sisters, and younger brother.

Although she only had a sixth-grade education, she managed to compensate for it with her worldly wisdom and a Ph.D. (which stands for Poor, Hungry, and Driven). My grandmother worked for years as a domestic in the homes of white people in the Old South, doing tasks such as washing, ironing, cooking, cleaning, and caring for their children. Among all the things she did for those families, it was her exceptional ability to care for their children that truly distinguished her. As a result, there was always a demand for her services because she was a trustworthy, dedicated, and skilled caregiver for children.

Her willingness to love another person's child unconditionally, as if that child were her own, enabled her to develop the reputation of being the best caregiver in the small town of Dublin, Georgia. Her reputation as an excellent caregiver also provided her with a reliable source of income to support her family. When times got tough and jobs were scarce, she always managed to secure employment due to her reputation. If she had been a basketball player, she would have been one of the first players picked on the playground. Her unique passing ability would have made her a player that everyone wanted to play with, because the way she would have played would have made everybody on her team a better player. If she had actually been a player, her mindset when it came to being a willing passer in the game of basketball was a life skill she embraced throughout her entire life. In her role as a caregiver, one of her notable clients was Dr. Cobb, the grandfather of the renowned Hall of Fame baseball player, Ty Cobb. She often looked after young Ty when he visited his grandfather's home.

While I can't say for certain whether her influence played a role in his legendary success, what I do know is that if he spent time with her, he would have encountered some of her profound life-changing words of wisdom. Particularly, she emphasized the importance of work ethic, having energy, passion, and a selfless concern for the well-being of others. Like many great players in the game of basketball and life, she understood her talent and how to use it best to WIN (be successful). Essentially, she knew how to *fit in, to get in*. She wouldn't have been a *Passer* secretly wanting to be a shooter or a rebounder; instead, she would have been happy with her role as a *Passer*. In other words, she knew what she did best and how to use it to her advantage to get into the *game* and stay in the *game* as it relates to the game of life. Now, looking back, I can clearly see what I couldn't see as a child,

14

even as a young adult. The wisdom mama *passed* on to me wasn't *sophisticated, complex,* or *hard to understand*. Rather, it was simply about *work ethic, education, communication skills, passion for what you do, and the will to see things through*. In her own way, she made sure I understood that I needed a life skill set, similar to having a skill set in the game of basketball. She believed that having a life skill set was necessary to compete successfully in the game of life, regardless of what I would eventually decide to do."

I thank God every day for my grandma because without her, I would have never developed the sound fundamental life skills that I needed to reach the level of success I have now. I have been a devoted husband to my wife Cynthia for 46 years, and I am the proud father of three lovely, well-adjusted adult children: Quentin, Simone, and Michael Ray. Additionally, I have been incredibly blessed to have a successful career as a basketball coach.

I'm not trying to imply that every day of my life has been free of life's trials and tribulations. However, what I am saying is that because of my grandma's wisdom, I was equipped to handle those challenges. She made sure I had the right set of life skills. My grandmother's *passes of wisdom* will echo forever into eternity through the lives of the many young men and women that I touched because of the life lessons she passed on to me. The wisdom she passed on to them through me will continuously be shared with future champions in the game of life who are yet unborn. If you don't catch any other *pass of wisdom* in this book, please grasp this one! The unselfishness of *Great Passer* like my grandmother rubs off on other people who eventually become unselfish themselves, adopting the characteristics of a *Great Passer*. This creates a culture of unselfishness in families, communities, churches, businesses, and our country. When this culture of unselfishness becomes a defining characteristic of any particular group of people, team, or organization, success becomes inevitable.

My grandmother was always my primary mentor until her death in 1987. I knew I could always trust her advice because she was a woman of great faith and foresight. As I mentioned earlier, she was determined until her last day to ensure that I had a solid foundation of life skills that would give me a fighting chance to succeed. However, when I began to actively search for a career path that would be my life's destiny. I realized that even if she were still alive, her guidance would not be applicable. The guidance I now needed, specifically on how to become a basketball coach, was beyond her area of expertise. Looking back, I believe she was well aware of this fact. I also believe she knew that once I started my actual career path, she would no longer be able to provide me with the guidance (passes) that would help me succeed (score) in whatever career path I chose. Obviously, coaching basketball turned out to be the career path of my choice. I'm not trying to diminish her years of insightful passes of knowledge and wisdom in the game of life. However, now it was time for me to find someone who would be willing to mentor me, teach me the intricacies of the game, and guide me in the right direction to become a successful basketball coach.

I believe that most basketball experts in today's game would agree that the fundamental skill of passing the basketball is a lost art. Many of them base this thought on the heightened selfish play connected to today's game. When you think about it, this selfish style of play is a repercussion of today's "me" society. Unfortunately, we're living in times when a lot of people (including players) are more concerned about themselves rather than others, including their teammates. This is why many players today prioritize their own self interests above all else. This toxic philosophy of "me" rather than "we" is self-centered and destructive. Unfortunately, this self-centered and destructive attitude has made its way into today's game of basketball.

16

Although I have to admit that, on occasion, there have been some teams that have been successful playing what I consider a selfish style of basketball. On the other hand, the facts show that the success of these teams is very fleeting and literally unsustainable. On the other hand, teams that have been able to sustain a high level of success over the years play a style of basketball that is totally contrary to the selfish style typically played in today's game. Teams like the San Antonio Spurs, Miami Heat, Milwaukee Bucks, and the Golden State Warriors who have won five NBA championships in the last eight seasons. Of those eight seasons, they lost in the final game of the championship series twice. I consider all of these teams to be NBA elite-level teams that consistently win year after year. In retrospect, the common denominator among all these teams is that they all play an unselfish style of basketball that utilizes the pass as the focal point of their offensive attack.

Great Passers in the game of basketball also possess incredible vision. They see opportunities for their teammates to score that ordinary players don't see. Often in the game of life, we need an assist from a Great Passer who can set us up to score (succeed) just as we would if we were playing basketball. Essentially, we need someone to give us guidance (a pass) that will put us on the road to success when we don't believe we're able to get there on our own. This person (Passer) becomes particularly important to us when life hits us with some form of adversity, hard times, or just one of life's plain old-fashioned ruts. Players in the game of basketball are no different from those of us playing the game of life. They, too, face adversity, such as a tough loss, a season-ending injury, reduced playing time, or something as simple as a shooting slump. Let me explain what a shooting slump entails. A shooting slump occurs when a player (or person) despite their best efforts, is unable to score a basket (or in other words succeed). In the game of life, slumps are no different from those in the game of basketball. Slumps in life can manifest in various forms, such as struggling to find a new job, dealing with health issues, or facing marital problems. In either case, whether it's life or basketball, if we're not careful, a slump can cause you to lose your hope, focus, and vision.

The Word of God defines *hope* as "the substance of things hoped for and the evidence of things unseen." Therefore, when a man or woman loses hope, their ability to maintain vision and focus becomes nearly impossible. Looking back at my own life, there was a time when I had lost all three: my hope, my vision, and my focus. Financial adversity hit me literally right between the eyes, blinding me to all my future aspirations, hopes, and dreams. My vision was so unclear during this time that even after I got out of my financial fix, I still could not see myself having any chance of achieving financial stability. I found myself developing a loser's mentality, a loser in the real game, *the game of life*. During that time, I wasn't a lazy guy; in fact, I had three jobs. Yet, I still felt as though I was moving further and further away from fulfilling my life's destiny. Although I had no idea what was supposed to be my life's destiny, deep down, I knew that I was capable of so much more than working the typical daily 9 to 5 job. This mentality is the source of ruts that so many people fall into when they feel all hope is gone. During that time, it seemed that no matter how hard I tried to change things, nothing worked. No matter what I did, things weren't changing. Because of this, I continued to feel like I was going nowhere, destined to live my life without ever realizing my life's true destiny. Then, I decided to honestly self-evaluate my life, which led me to realize that I wasn't adequately prepared to compete in the game of life successfully. Looking back, that honest self-evaluation was the beginning of my life's breakthrough.

The ability to self-evaluate is the first step to embarking on the right road to success. Unfortunately, honest self-evaluation is something that most of us struggle with. If you're not willing to admit to yourself, "I'm not good enough," "I need to improve," or

"I can give more effort," then don't expect to achieve significant success. When you find yourself stuck in a rut, drifting further away from your goals and dreams, it's crucial to recognize that breaking through the stagnation requires an honest evaluation of yourself and your situation. If you're the type of person who struggles with honest self-evaluation, then you'll need the assistance of a great PASSER. "Because great passers in the game of life have the vision needed to put you in a position to succeed. The reason their insight is so valuable is that they can see things in you that you can't see in yourself."

As fate would have it, the next great passer in my life turned out to be my college teammate, coaching mentor, and friend, Tom Izzo. The fall of 1973 marked my second year at Northern Michigan University and the first time I met Tom Izzo. I encountered him when Tom and Steve Mariucci, two snotty-nosed freshmen, were attempting to navigate their way around campus. They approached me for directions, unaware that they were standing right in front of the building they were looking for. How ironic it was that I first crossed paths with Tom and Steve as they were trying to find their way to an unfamiliar place. If you trace their career trajectories, starting from college, you'll discover that both of them had less than a one in two million chance of attaining the level of professional success they both have achieved today.

The point I'm trying to make here can be better explained with this simple but profound quote: *"You must make or create your own path."* A few years back, my wife Cynthia and I were on vacation in the Upper Peninsula of Michigan. The first thing I noticed right away was something that had not changed since I was last there as a student at NMU. One of the unique characteristics of people in the U.P. is that they make or create their own walking paths, regardless of whether there are already sidewalks or roads already in place. I think this attitude has a subconscious effect on how people in the U.P. approach their lives.

In my opinion, they're the type of people who make their own pathway. Evidence of this can be found in the "rags to riches" life stories of Tom and Steve, two individuals from Iron Mountain, a small town located in the northwestern region of Michigan's Upper Peninsula. Iron Mountain is a mining town with a population of probably no more than 2,000 people. Most of the town's residents work in the mines throughout the year until it becomes too cold to continue. During the winter months, they often rely on unemployment benefits while they wait for spring to return and resume their work in the mines.

How Tom and Steve were able to develop the mindset necessary to envision themselves as the successful coaches they are today is truly remarkable. It highlights the incredible power of dreaming big and having the courage to pursue those dreams in the face of seemingly insurmountable challenges. Steve has enjoyed a distinguished career in the NFL, serving as the head coach of the San Francisco 49ers and currently earning immense respect as a commentator on the NFL network. On the other hand, Tom has achieved numerous milestones throughout his basketball career, earning him a well-deserved place in the basketball Hall of Fame alongside the greatest coaches in the history of the game of basketball.

Of all the people I've had the opportunity to spend time with, there isn't one person other than my grandmother who has the intestinal fortitude to fight against unimaginable odds like Chief (Tom Izzo). When he arrived on campus, he had no scholarship, but when he left, he had turned himself into an All-American and a three-year captain of our team.

To understand how he developed his intense intestinal drive, you need to know a little bit about his background and who he may have taken some of his most influential passes from without even realizing it. Of course both of his parents, Carl and Dorothy, played a significant role in shaping Tom's life. But I was always fascinated by the stories Chief would tell me about his grandfather, Tony Izzo, who was an Italian immigrant and a shoe cobbler in their town of Iron Mountain. It's an occupation that I'm sure doesn't even exist today. The job of a shoe cobbler was to repair damaged shoes, often by putting new heels and soles on them. In those days, almost every town in the country had a shoe cobbler's shop because most people couldn't afford to simply buy a new pair of shoes when theirs were worn out or damaged. Chief said Tony worked in his shoe shop until the day he died at the age of ninety-something. Tom once told me that he remembers Tony working in his shop countless hours, even at an elderly age, working all day and night until he was too tired to continue. In fact, rather than leave the shop, he would go to a room in the back and lie down on a little sleeping cot until he was rested enough to continue working. Tony's commitment to his work describes the work ethic of his grandson, Tom Izzo, perfectly. Comparatively, Tommy's grandfather, like my grandmother, was a great example of what work ethic, intense drive, and determination can achieve if you're willing to endure life's hardships, trials, and tribulations. I don't know if Tom even realizes the impact his grandfather's eternal passes had on him in terms of his success as a basketball coach. I believe that the mere fact that Chief saw Tony's work ethic and perseverance every day, whether subconsciously or consciously, imprinted a picture in his mind that patience, persistence, and work ethic are all part of the process of living a successful life.

As good friends, Tom and I kept in close touch with each other throughout our time apart after college. Therefore, I knew all about the hardships he had to endure as he went through the evolution of his coaching career. I know for a fact that there were some really hard times, many of which not many people could have managed to get through. Over the years, I've had people say to me that they would give anything to be Tom Izzo. My first response is always the same, "Are you sure?" Then I ask them if they'd be willing to spend seven years of their life dwelling in the desert without any guarantee that they would ever reach the promised land. Most of them respond with a look of confusion because they have no idea what I really mean.

Throughout my life, I've met a lot of very talented people who are well-equipped with everything it takes to be success stories. However, 99% of them lack the resilience required to succeed because they don't possess what it takes to endure the challenges of life without giving up. The "desert" in Tom's life refers to the seven years he spent making very little to no money, working endless hours as the lowest-ranking member on Jud Heathcote's staff at Michigan State. During those years, he slept on a mattress in the basement of a college classmate from Northern Michigan because he couldn't afford a place of his own. Throughout that time, he never heard a word of encouragement, gratitude, or appreciation for a job well done. He was told repeatedly to quit and that he wasn't cut out to be a coach. Meanwhile, he had to endure the emotional and mental stress brought on by the doubt and uncertainty that there would be better times ahead of him in the future. Yet through it all, he never lost his hope or the necessary focus and vision needed to see his dream of one day becoming a head basketball coach come true. Tom's success has always been predicated on one particular mindset throughout his entire career, which has been to be a passer for other people, seeking life-changing success. He has essentially created a Hall of Fame career for himself from his pass-first mindset that puts the goals and dreams of other people ahead of his own.

A fail-safe mindset that I wholeheartedly believe in myself. I truly believe that the pass-first mindset brings back reciprocal measures of success throughout your entire life. As I previously

22

mentioned, I want to reiterate that great passers in the game of basketball have great vision; they see scoring opportunities that other players (people) don't see. The same is true when it pertains to the vision of great passers in the game of life. Tom's great vision made him one of those great passers during his playing days at NMU, and he has been able to translate his great passing skills into a life-changing skill in the game of life. Years ago, as a youngster, Chief envisioned his own success long before it ever happened.

I often thank God that He made me a part of what Tom envisioned his success would look like. When we were eighteen-year-old college teammates, Tom convinced me to make a promise to him while we were sitting in the tail end of a six-passenger prop plane; that I would come and work for him if he ever became a head college basketball coach. I recall that we were on our way to play against Western Illinois University. It was one of the few times we flew because, in those days, when you played Division II ball like we did, every trip was by bus due to budget constraints. I remember the conversation vividly, as if it were yesterday. Tom shared his future plans of becoming a great basketball coach and expressed his intention to hire me as his assistant coach when he achieved that goal. I waited until he was done talking to let him know that I had no intentions of being a coach and, furthermore, what would I look like working for him. At that point, he Izzo'd me, but before he did, he asked me what I wanted to do if I didn't want to coach basketball. I told him I wanted to be a businessman and make all the money in the world. Then he hit me with this Izzo, saying, "Ok then, you go and make all the money in the world, and then you can come work for me without having to worry about money." I reiterated to him what would I look like working for him. He Izzo'd me again, unwilling to take no for an answer. He then said, "Okay, then I'll work for you, depending on who becomes a head coach first, you or me."

This conversation speaks volumes about his ability to see in me what I couldn't see in myself, which was his belief that I could be a basketball coach. He persisted until I promised him that I would coach with him if he ever became a head coach. Exhausted by his persistence, I finally agreed. Little did I know that one day I would be called upon to fulfill that promise, which happened twenty-five years later on a hot, sunny afternoon in late July. I vividly remember that day because I had just finished an exhausting two weeks of coaching at the Five Star Basketball Camp. When I arrived home that afternoon, I noticed that the grass in my yard had grown over a foot high during my extended absence. When I pulled into the driveway, I went straight into the garage and immediately took out the lawn mower, fully intending to mow the grass. However, I was quickly distracted once inside the house by the prospect of a short, refreshing nap.

Several hours later, as fate would have it, I was awakened by a phone call. My first instinct was to let it ring. After all, I was tired and trying to rest. But the thought that it could be my wife and kids wouldn't allow me to ignore the call. To my surprise, when I picked it up, it was Tom. In his usual manner, he started the conversation by greeting me as he always does, saying, "Mike-Iz. What's going on?" My reply was, "I'm so tired I can't see straight; just got in from Five Star." He then asked me if I had time to ride with him to Detroit. The reason for his trip was that he was on his way to watch an AAU practice at Bishop Borgess High School. He mentioned that he had some things to talk to me about, and because I sensed the urgency in his voice, I immediately asked him what this was all about. He began talking about our glory days back at Northern Michigan and reminded me of the promise we had made to one another nearly 25 years ago in the back of our six-seat prop plane headed to play a game at Western Illinois. That's when he revealed to me that he was set to be the next Head Coach at Michigan State. Immediately, I started to laugh in disbelief and begged him to get serious and

24

tell me what was up. He laughed and replied, "NO BS! I'm going to be the next head guy at State." I started laughing again. Then he Izzo'd me once more, hitting me with the perfect question to make sure I took him seriously. "So, what are you and Cynthia doing this Sunday?" At that moment, I said to him, "You're serious, aren't you? You're going to be the next head coach at Michigan State?" I then said, "Come and get me so we can talk."

When Tom arrived at my place, he began explaining what had happened and how he had indeed become the next head coach at Michigan State. During his explanation, he mentioned that the Board of Trustees had voted and approved his appointment in a closed-door meeting, excluding the public and media. Their plan was to have him in place before Jud Heathcote retired after the upcoming season. He then reaffirmed, as if no time had passed since that fateful day 25 years ago, that he still intended to include me as part of his staff.

This particular experience taught me a valuable life lesson, one that I often share with my audience whenever I have the opportunity to speak publicly. Whether the audience consists of young or old people, men or women, it doesn't matter. I always stress the importance of genuine relationships and how a single relationship can be the breakthrough that ultimately changes your life. I know this to be true because my amazing career as a basketball coach is a direct result of the relationship I established with Tom when I was an eighteen-year-old snotty-nosed kid. Often, we overlook how the good Lord, who is the greatest passer of all times, puts certain passers (people) into our lives who deliver his divine purpose for our lives. Looking back, I've come to realize that Mama Seed and Tom Izzo were the passers that the Lord intended to miraculously change my life.

In summary *Passing* a basketball effectively in the game of basketball is similar to making accurate and timely decisions in life. *Passing* the basketball ball requires careful observation, awareness, and delivery. It is important that the *Passer* recognize the strengths and weaknesses of teammates, anticipating their movements, and delivering the ball precisely to ensure a scoring opportunity. Similarly, in life, we encounter situations where we need to assess the strengths and weaknesses of those around us, understand their needs, and offer support or assistance accordingly. This parallel between basketball and life highlights the significance of understanding the value of passing.

Overall, the skill of passing in basketball serves as a metaphor for the valuable skills required in navigating life. By recognizing the similarities between basketball passes and life's decisions, we can cultivate wisdom and enhance our ability to connect with and support others. So, let us appreciate the seemingly simple act of passing a basketball and understand its profound implications for a successful and fulfilling life.

Fundamental #2 Dribbling

Mateen Cleaves

Throughout my life, I've often heard people say that when you name a baby, you should give your child a name that you believe they can live up to, and most of the time, they will live up to that name. When Herb and Francis Cleaves decided to name their son Mateen, which means "powerful warrior," there is no doubt that they rightfully named him.

Of all the players I've had the opportunity to coach, Mateen is by far the one player who embodies what it means to be a high-performance maximum execution player. There was never a day, whether it was practice or a game, that he didn't strive to execute at a high-performance maximum level of play. When I had my first opportunity to meet Mateen, he was with his mother, Francis, who had driven him to campus in May of 1996.

That day Tom asked me to meet them right outside the arena doors at gate B. The reason he asked me in particular was because not only did he want me to meet Mateen but he also knew that I would do it without feeling like he was asking me to be a doorman. In those days our offices were downstairs which meant we had no way of knowing when our guests would actually get to the arena doors. If there was no one upstairs to let them inside they had to call our office and stand there waiting until someone made it upstairs to let them in the building.

The other reason he wanted me to get to know Mateen ASAP was that one of the first things we talked about when he hired me was that he wanted Mateen and me to be "connected at the hip," as he likes to say. This was because Mateen would be incredibly valuable to the future success of our team. When Mateen and his mother, Francis, arrived and stepped out of the car, walking towards the building, I immediately noticed that Francis was more than just Mateen's mother; she was indeed a special woman. Every step she took was accompanied by the aura of an African queen. Her undeniable self-confidence, pride, and dignity were evident in the Afrocentric attire she wore that day. Francis had to drive Mateen to campus because he didn't have a driver's license or his own car. In fact, he never took the time to attend the necessary driver's education classes required to obtain a license because he didn't want to take time off from his workout routine because he was dedicated to becoming the best basketball player possible.

After we all introduced ourselves, the three of us went downstairs to our offices where Tom was waiting for us. Once we made our way to the office, there were a few minutes of idle conversation. Then Tom asked Francis if he could have a moment to speak with Mateen alone. While Tom and Mateen were talking, I invited Francis to wait in my office until Tom was done speaking to Mateen because he wanted to speak with her alone as well. Once in my office, we immediately started a conversation about the social ills of the black community. We both agreed that it was important for black men to be positive role models for young black boys. Then our conversation shifted to the overall social ills of our country. During that shift in conversation, she conveyed to me one of the most profound statements I've ever heard regarding the horrific grip of social injustice. She said that this particular aspect of social injustice would one day affect every single person in the entire country, regardless of race, religion, or misleading societal entitlement. The only exception might be a select group of people who could protect themselves because of their wealth and social status. Here's exactly what she said to me, "When a nation purposely creates laws to criminalize its citizens, that nation is on the brink of collapse."

She said that to me back in 1996, and right now, today in 2023, we are witnessing in real time the realities of her words. Francis was obviously an intelligent woman, but even more importantly, she was a wise woman who understood the importance of sharing her knowledge and wisdom with her children because she wanted them to grow up to be effective, impactful leaders in society. The leadership skills Mateen learned from her most certainly made an everlasting impact on the Michigan State basketball program because it was his leadership that was the key to restoring our program back to national prominence and winning the 2000 national championship. Contrary to what most people think, effective leadership is driven by relationships. It amounts to more than just God-given talent, but rather, its qualities are most often the result of an upbringing steeped in the value of leadership as a service to the greater good of society as a whole. Mateen's upbringing was just that way. He often shared with me on several occasions that his parents would have him and his siblings sit through school board meetings, city council board meetings, and any other local civically active group meetings that could possibly affect the welfare of their community. He said that growing up, he learned from watching his parents how important leadership was in terms of getting a group of people to all work together to bring about successful outcomes. He went on to say that his parents continuously stressed to him that his parents continuously stress that success of any kind is hinged on effective relationship-driven leadership, whether that be in a business boardroom or on the basketball court.

That day, Mateen and Francis's purpose for their trip was to drop him off for summer school because he was enrolled in a program called SUPER. It was a academic program designed to give students a head start on the academic challenges that most incoming freshmen would face. Back then, the only way to have an incoming freshman on campus during the summer without them paying their own money was to get them enrolled in an academic program specifically designed to enrich their academic skills in preparation for college. That's exactly what the SUPER program was set up to do, and the director, Betty Sanford, was a tough, no-nonsense disciplinarian and success-driven woman who wouldn't accept anything less than a high-performance, maximum execution effort from every student in her program, regardless of who they were. She didn't care if it was Nick Saban's star freshman running back, Sedrick Irvin, in football, or if it was Tom Izzo's 5-star point guard, Mateen Cleaves, in basketball. As students in the program, they were going to adhere to her rules, do their work, and behave themselves appropriately. Initially, we had no idea how intense the program would be or what Mateen would be in store for throughout the eight-week program. Betty was a tough taskmaster, but she sincerely had Mateen's, as well as every kid in her program, best interests at heart. She would always say to me when referring to Mateen, "There's so much potential there, so much potential, Coach. He has so much more to offer than just his basketball abilities."

The following pages of this chapter will demonstrate how Mateen utilized the same thought processes and fundamental skills to master dribbling to navigate his way through some of the most critical times of his career. As one of college basketball's greatest ball handlers, Mateen was an extremely skillful dribbler and has successfully translated those dribbling skills into life skills, that enabling him to become a great handler of his dreams and goals. Dribbling and passing are basketball skills categorized as ball handling. They are similar in their importance in playing the game of basketball effectively. Ball handlers need to be very skillful dribblers and passers because it is their job to take care of the basketball without making mistakes that would turn the ball over to the other team. The ball handler is more important than any other player on the team because possession of the ball is key to playing winning basketball. If the ball handler is not capable of effectively dribbling and passing the ball, they won't be able to create scoring opportunities for their teammates.

The dribble itself is the method used to advance the ball from one area of the playing floor to another when the ball handler can't pass the ball ahead to another teammate. The ball handler can also use the dribble as a strategy to maneuver around defensive players to score a basket themselves or create a scoring opportunity for another teammate.

Comparatively, in the game of life, dribbling equates to the act of birthing a new idea into existence. Opportunities to succeed in life are no different than those in basketball. The value of a great ball handler to a winning team is priceless. Similarly, to win in the game of life, you must be a great handler of your goals and dreams.

Great ball handlers in the game of basketball are proficient in all of the following three basic fundamentals of dribbling: 1) They always dribble with the ball out in front of them. 2) They always dribble with their head up.3) They always dribble with their body in a ready-to-play basketball position.

If you want to be a great handler of your goals and dreams, you must be proficient in the same basic fundamentals, as they pertain to the game of life:1) You must always keep your goals and dreams in front of you. 2) You must keep your head up so that you can see opportunities to fulfill your goals and dreams.3) You must stay in a ready-to-play position, which translates into being ready both mentally and physically to carry out whatever is necessary to fulfill your goals and dreams when the opportunity presents itself.

"Mateen Cleaves was the preeminent player amongst an elite group responsible for ushering in the legendary era of Michigan State basketball under Tom Izzo. Mateen's leadership, infectious smile, and exceptional ball-handling skills propelled us to heights previously unknown to Michigan State basketball prior to his arrival on campus in the fall of 1996. Our three consecutive Big Ten championships and back-to-back Final Fours, culminating in a National Championship in 2000, surpass the accomplishments of any other Spartan player to this day. By the end of his tenure at Michigan State, Mateen had achieved every conceivable dream for his college career. However, the road to realizing those goals and dreams was not easy. The journey was filled with hardships, trials, and tribulations, with a career steeped in uncertainty from its inception. His story is one of overcoming insurmountable odds to quite literally snatch victory from the jaws of self-defeat."

The day Mateen arrived on the Michigan State campus, he was already heralded as the best player since Magic Johnson to wear a Spartan uniform. He came in as a McDonald's All-American, the top-ranked freshman point guard in the country, and was predicted to be the Big Ten Freshman Player of the Year. He was also burdened with the prospect of immediately bringing Michigan State back into basketball prominence nationally. However, his immediate success was hindered by a serious back injury from playing high school football, which was further aggravated in a rollover automobile accident while on his recruiting visit to the University of Michigan. Unfortunately, all of this happened before he even arrived on campus. To this day, most fans don't know the full extent of Mateen's injury or the fact that he played his entire freshman year in a plastic body cast. The cast was specifically designed to press down on his testicles to keep him from bending over too far while he played.

The idea behind this was to prevent any further injuries to his back while attempting to play during the healing process. If he had re-injured his back in his attempt to play while injured, it would have destroyed any chances for him to have a meaningful college or professional basketball career. Incidentally, the Michigan State basketball program would have never become what it is today.

Mateen demonstrated his true resolve when he decided to play regardless of his physical condition, when most players would have sat out the year. Both he and his parents, Herb and Frances Cleaves, along with Coach Izzo, made the gutsy decision to have him play through his injury. As I recall, going into the meeting, Tom and his parents were concerned that Mateen might not be able to handle the prospect of sitting out the season, but sitting out would have probably been best for him. Somehow during that meeting, Mateen convinced both his parents and Chief that it would be in his best interest to play regardless of his injury. Mateen told me that he was able to persuade them by convincing them that not playing would damage his chances of playing professional basketball in the future. Ultimately, they agreed because he was able to further convince them that professional teams would consider him "damaged goods." In his mind, it would be better to play while injured and risk not performing well, rather than sitting out the entire year with everyone questioning the seriousness of his injury. There were also other factors that influenced Mateen's eagerness to play right away. The prospect of playing with lifelong friends Antonio Smith and Morris

Peterson, who both also influenced his decision to come to Michigan State in the first place, played a significant role. The three had played together and against each other as youth in and around their hometown of Flint, Michigan. It had always been the dream of all three guys to play together, along with their younger friend Charlie Bell, who arrived on campus one year later. They formed the legendary foursome known in the basketball world as the Flintstones.

The four of them would manufacture an era of basketball unprecedented in the 120-year history of Michigan State basketball. Mateen, cognizant of his teammates, knew from the beginning that their likelihood of winning without him would be minimal because he was the straw that stirred the drink. Although he was injured, he was not going to let his teammates down, even though he clearly understood that if he re-injured his back, it could put an end to his playing career altogether. The fact that he was willing to jeopardize his entire playing career earned him instant credibility, unconditional love, loyalty, and the trust of every player on our team. As a result, they all believed he was the guy who would eventually lead them to the promised land of college basketball.

The unique ability to apply skills learned in one stage of life, such as dribbling a basketball, can be a powerful tool when it comes to another stage of life—provided that you are mindful enough to recognize the similarities between the two. For instance, I believe that Mateen Cleaves would have struggled to overcome a very challenging period in his basketball career if he had not understood the parallels between the skills he acquired while playing basketball, starting from his youth gaining the knowledge of how those skills could effectively be utilized to overcome difficult times in life. Like all great ball handlers in the game of basketball, Mateen understood the importance of following the three fundamental skills of dribbling a basketball. The first is always to keep the ball out in front of you, especially when pressured by a trapping defense. Secondly, always dribble with your head up, and third, always dribble with your body in a ready-to-play basketball position. These fundamental dribbling skills, when thoughtfully utilized in the game of basketball, can also translate into life skills that promote effective management of handling circumstances that can negatively impact your goals and dreams in both basketball and life.

During some of the toughest times in his basketball career, Mateen Cleaves used the same thought processes needed to successfully dribble the basketball against a challenging defender to effectively keep his goals and dreams in the game of life in front of him.

Fortunately for us he had the thoughtfulness to realize that he could utilize his past experiences playing basketball and translate those experiences into thought processes he would need to keep the ball (his goals and dreams) of one day winning the National Championship in front of him, despite his troubling back injury. The ability to effectively translate what you've learned from past experiences and turn them into useful knowledge that can help you through current circumstances can be beneficial throughout your entire life. In order to someday fulfill his goals and dreams, Mateen realized that he would eventually have to utilize the thought process needed to dribble a basketball effectively to protect his dreams and goals against overwhelming odds. He would have to effectively maneuver around the challenging obstacles he was currently facing in the game of life.

The Mateen Cleaves life-changing story demonstrates how these analogies of life and basketball can be very valuable life changing tools. To begin with, he used the first fundamental skill of dribbling the basketball, which is to keep the ball (your dreams) in front of you. This analogy came into play when he had to utilize the thought process needed to dribble a basketball effectively as a life skill, in order to convince Tom and his parents that it would be in his best interest to play his freshman year regardless of his back injury.

The second basic fundamental skill of dribbling the basketball, which is a skill mastered by all great ball handlers, is to dribble the ball with your head up. One of Mateen's best attributes as a player was his ability to see the play develop long before it actually happened. When this skill is translated into the game of life, it equates to being able to anticipate the chance for great opportunities. This is why the thought process needed to effectively dribble the ball with your head up is a significant factor in recognizing opportunities for success in the game of life.

As a result, numerous basketball players fail to perceive developing plays due to their failure to keep their heads up while dribbling. Regrettably, this pattern often persists once their playing days are behind them, hindering their transition to a successful life. Fundamentally, their inability to recognize the significance of maintaining awareness prevents them from seizing opportunities to score and succeed, resulting in missed chances for success in the game of life.

When Mateen successfully convinced his parents and Tom to let him play. He was then faced with the reality of what it would take to prepare himself for the game. In order to compete at the Big Ten level and perform at his best, he needed a plan that emphasized the third aspect of being a great dribbler; which is to maintain a low body position while playing basketball. This mindset of effective dribbling also translated into being prepared to seize opportunities in life. To succeed in life, one must be physically and mentally prepared to tackle the daily struggles, stresses, and challenges that come with it. Mateen confronted the harsh reality that the season was rapidly approaching, and he hadn't engaged in any playing or conditioning for the past seven months. When confronted with these two challenges, he understood that he would need to build up significant physical and mental strength in order to adequately prepare himself for college basketball, especially considering the long period of inactivity he had experienced.

The book of Proverbs, chapter 18, verse 24 in the Bible states, "A man of many friends will prove himself a bad friend, but there will be a friend who sticks to him closer than a brother." This Bible verse highlights the significance of great teammates, who are akin to loyal and supportive friends, especially during challenging times. True friends are not always concerned with telling you what you want to hear, but rather provide you with honest advice that you need to hear. Antonio Smith exemplifies this kind of friend, and his role as Mateen's teammate was crucial for the difficulties that lay ahead. Having been friends since childhood, Tonio and Mateen's deep bond influenced Mateen's decision to join Michigan State. Antonio's support for Mateen involved a combination of tough love and holding him accountable for achieving his best possible physical condition within a limited timeframe. However, a major obstacle arose as Mateen was under doctor's orders to refrain from any physical activity until the first day of practice on October 15th.

All athletes are familiar with their own bodies, and Mateen was well aware of his physical condition. He recognized that without some form of conditioning, it would be impossible to achieve anything during the season. Mateen faced a two-fold challenge: recovering from an injury and having limited time to regain his fitness. It would have been nearly impossible to overcome the daunting task of getting back in shape after nearly a year of inactivity, even for a warrior as strong-willed and determined as Mateen Cleaves. However, thanks to the unwavering love and support of his accountability partner, Antonio Smith, who stood by him day after day, week after week, and month after month, Mateen was able to rise above these obstacles.

Shortly after deciding that Mateen would attempt to play, both he and Antonio unexpectedly visited my office. From their body language alone, it was evident that they had something important to discuss. Little did I know, that discussion would involve me. As they took their seats, they began expressing concerns about Mateen's injury and how it would be impossible for him to play unless he got into shape. As the conversation unfolded, I unknowingly found myself agreeing to something that I probably shouldn't have, especially without talking to Chief and our team doctor. If Mateen would have further injured himself while working out with Tonio and me, Chief would have had no choice but to fire me. Due to the potential for further damage to his injured back, which could have resulted in a career-ending injury or even worse, all three of us - Antonio, Mateen, and myself - were aware that disregarding the doctor's orders was a significant risk. We understood that this decision had the potential to ruin Mateen's entire life. However, the driving force behind our actions was Mateen's unwavering desire to play and his trust in Antonio and myself.

That afternoon in my office, I gained valuable insight into each young mans character. We shared a common trait: a genuine commitment to helping others. I believe that this characteristic is key to achieving success. The bond between these two individuals was unlike anything I had ever witnessed before. The heartfelt words they expressed in my office convinced me that I was willing to take a chance on them, even though the possibility of losing my job would be hanging over my head.

To accomplish Mateen's objectives, they understood the importance of having a plan and me as a capable accountability partner to execute it. Despite being new to the team, they believed I was the right person for the task. Later that day, both of them visited my office to discuss the schedule for our workouts in the practice gym. After careful consideration, we agreed to meet at 5:00 AM. Our early start would help us avoid detection by other coaches and anyone else who might reveal our plans. The following Monday, at the agreed time, both of them arrived eagerly, ready to start our workout. However, I immediately noticed Mateen's demeanor displaying some hesitation. In an attempt to offer reassurance, I simply said, "At least you'll know." He nodded in agreement. Then we began the work, only to realize quickly that the battle ahead was tougher than anyone had anticipated. It was disheartening to see Moe struggle to get his body to cooperate. Even doing a simple lay-up drill or running across the court was difficult due to the severe pain in his back. I remember attempting a drill where he had to run to the free throw line, turn around, and run back to touch the rim. Normally, this is a great conditioning exercise, but Moe couldn't even jump high enough to reach the rim at that point. So, I suggested he try touching the bottom of the backboard, but he couldn't do that either. As a last resort, I asked him to touch the bottom of the net, but once again, he failed.

While it was a disappointing day for Moe's conditioning progress, it was also a day of clarity as we now understood the magnitude of the challenges ahead.

After the workout, I spoke to Moe and made a promise. I told him that if he was willing to continue trying, I would come up with a better plan for him the next day. That night, I took some time for reflection and prayer. The following morning, I felt confident in my new plan. Before we began, I explained to both Tonio and Mateen that the new plan would be simple. We would progress gradually, taking baby steps at first. My idea was to go back to the basics of basketball, starting with the ABC's of the game. We started with drills that focused on breaking down the fundamental skills of the game, such as layups, shooting, passing, and dribbling. We approached these skills in their simplest forms, just as one would teach a child starting from scratch. I also had another thought regarding Mateen. I believed that we should let his body guide us in determining when, what, and how much we could do with him.

38

I discussed this with Tonio, and we both agreed that it was the best approach. We knew that Mateen had a strong desire to play and that he would be the best judge of how far he could push himself.

The first workout provided us with valuable lessons. As a result, I decided to initiate each drill within the first quarter length of the basketball court, which extends from the out-of-bounds line to the top of the three-point line at the key. Once Moe was ready, we progressed to the half court line. Subsequently, we worked within three quarters of the court until we were able to utilize the entire length of the court. To give you an idea of Moe's starting point, imagine this: he struggled to run, not sprint, from the out-of-bounds line to the three-point line at the top of the key and back. Both Mateen and Antonio firmly believed that their unconditional love and shared belief in each other could conquer any pain, hardship, or setback. It was this very unconditional love and belief that motivated Mateen to persevere through the intense pain of a crippling back injury, regain his fitness, and play through the season, regardless of the injury's severity.

Most players wouldn't have played, but most players aren't Mateen Cleaves, nor could they ever be. That's because they lack his resolve, passion, and unrelenting determination. These three characteristics not only helped him overcome the darkest hours of his basketball career but also drove him to achieve three consecutive Big 10 Championships, two Final Fours, and a National Championship, all with his loyal Flintstone friends by his side.

Mateen's story vividly illustrates how the fundamental thought processes involved in effectively dribbling a basketball are also essential for overcoming the challenges posed by a full-court press defense in basketball. These same dribbling skills and thought processes are equally necessary for navigating setbacks, confrontations, and failures in life. I understand that some readers may find this analogy difficult to grasp if they are unfamiliar with the concept of a full-court press in basketball. To clarify, let me provide a more detailed explanation. Imagine that Mateen's injury represents the formidable full-court press defense that one can encounter in the game of life. Without the necessary dribbling skills, the full-court press of life would have trapped Mateen's dreams (symbolized by the ball) and forced him into failure, ultimately extinguishing any chance of realizing his aspirations and goals.

However, Mateen Cleaves was determined to fulfill his dreams despite his circumstances. As a skilled ball handler, he used his abilities to overcome life's challenges, just as he would to navigate through a pressure defense on the basketball court. The lessons he learned from playing basketball throughout his entire life empowered him to conquer similar circumstances in the game of life. If you aspire to achieve great things and live your dreams you will inevitably face obstacles that can potentially shatter those dreams. When such a situation arises, keep in mind that you can employ the same analogy of effectively dribbling a basketball to overcome the full-court press in the game of basketball. To overcome life challenging obstacles that could shatter your dreams and goals.

Fundamental #3 Shooting

Morris (Mo Pete) Peterson

#42. A jersey number that will never be worn again at Michigan State University, retired in honor of one of the best shooters in program history. This shooter played a significant role in our team's storied journey to Michigan State's second National Championship. It was late March in 2000, in chilly Auburn Hills, Michigan. On that day, Morris Peterson was the hero. It was the biggest game of "Pete's" college career, and it happened to be on the biggest stage in college basketball. That day, Pete made big shot after big shot to lead our team back to the Final Four for the second year in a row and give us a chance to eventually win the 2000 college basketball National Championship.

However, his greatest day would soon turn into his darkest night. After the game, the team celebrated on the court and then proceeded to the locker room, as per our usual post-game routine. But this time, things were different. Mo Pete's family joined us in the locker room to deliver the devastating news of his grandmother's passing. Pete and Chief were not present at that moment due to post-game interviews. I vividly remember that just as the family began explaining what had happened, Chief entered the room, followed shortly after by Pete, who wore a beaming smile on his face, proud of our achievement. However, that sense of joy stemming from our victory quickly dissipated as soon as Pete glanced at our expressions and read the distress in our body language. It was then that his mother, Valerie, spoke to Pete with a sorrowful expression on her face. "Baby Big Mama has passed away." At that moment, Pete broke down in tears, overcome with grief. I remember each player walking over to Pete, offering empathetic hugs and words of condolence. As our players and staff continued to console Pete, his family began to explain that during the very same moments when Morris secured our victory with his outstanding shooting exhibition, Pete's beloved grandmother, Clara Mae, had passed away.

Despite just winning the Midwest Regional championship and earning a spot in the 2000 college basketball final four, there was no thought of celebration. It was no longer about basketball; our focus shifted to supporting Pete and his family. After about half an hour, Tom instructed Matt Larson, our Sports Information Director (SID), to allow the media into our locker room. I'm certain Matt informed a few local reporters about Pete's grandmother's death, but it was evident that many, especially the national reporters, were unaware of the situation until they entered our locker room.

The guys who were interviewed didn't talk much about the game. Instead, they quickly shifted the conversation towards Pete because they knew how much he loved his grandmother. It was evident to everyone in the room that he was deeply affected by her loss. Many reporters had intended to interview Pete due to his exceptional shooting performance in the game. However, he was in no mental or emotional condition to face the media. He retreated to the shower room before they could reach him and stayed there until the last reporter left the locker room.

It was at that moment that I realized how long he had been in the shower. Concerned, I went back to check on him. I found him standing there, his tears mixing with the water from the shower. I tried to urge him, saying, "Come on, big fella, we have to go," but it seemed like he didn't hear me. Deciding not to bother him, I returned to the locker room and informed Tom that I couldn't get Pete out of the shower. Without hesitation, Tom went straight back to the shower room. He walked in with all his clothes on, even as the water continued to run, and embraced Pete. Then he said to him in these exact words, "This will be one of the toughest things you'll ever do," referring to the task of burying his grandmother. He also told him, "I'm here for you, whatever you need or decide to do. If you don't want to play, I understand." Pete then rested his head on Tom's shoulder and continued to cry. A few minutes later, they left the shower room. Pete got dressed and rode home to Flint with his parents, while the rest of us boarded the bus to return to East Lansing.

The bus ride back to East Lansing that night from the palace was somber, to say the least. I remember there were very few, if any, conversations throughout the entire journey. It felt as though we had lost the game. Under normal circumstances, we would have rocked the bus all the way back to East Lansing. When we arrived, Tom dismissed the team from the locker room as he usually does, without acknowledging what we had just accomplished in Auburn Hills that night.

Now, as we faced Wisconsin in the Final Four, the news about Pete's grandmother became public, causing a wave of unease and apprehension among Spartan Nation. We were up against the challenge of defeating the Badgers for the fourth time that season, a task that basketball experts claimed would be extremely difficult, as it's notoriously challenging to beat a team three times, let alone four times. On top of that, Pete's heart was understandably broken, making the feat seem nearly impossible. However, what the outside world didn't know was that our team had a history of finding strength and unity in the face of tragic circumstances. The emotional roller coaster we had experienced in the previous game had already brought our close-knit team even closer together. It had given a group of players who were already playing for each other an additional reason to win: Clara Mae.

In the game of basketball, it's widely believed that great shooters need great passers. They need someone who can deliver the ball to them when they want it, where they want it, and how they want it. Fortunately for us and Pete, he had two exceptional passers on his side. One was his teammate and lifelong friend, Mateen Cleaves, and the other was his coach, Tom Izzo. Given the circumstances, both Mateen and Chief knew that we had no chance of winning on Saturday against Wisconsin unless our best shooter was in the right frame of mind.

However, what the world still doesn't know is how deeply Pete was affected by his grandmother Clara Mae's passing. Their relationship was incredibly close, and Pete was overwhelmed by grief to the point where he briefly considered not playing against Wisconsin. It was only through the persuasive words of his mother, Val Peterson, who insisted that Clara Mae would have wanted him to play, that Pete ultimately decided to play. Furthermore, the encouragement and support he received from Mateen Cleaves and Tom were instrumental in helping him mentally prepare and deliver his best performance, leading to the 2000 Michigan State national championship.

During the following week, both Chief and Mateen's approach to helping Pete was *relationship leadership* focused. They immediately began the process of preparing Pete mentally for the upcoming game on Saturday. Although I don't know the exact words they used, one thing is certain: they both knew the significance of spending time with Pete, as it is often the most meaningful gesture for someone who is grieving. The days ahead were bound to be some of the most challenging in Pete's life. He was going to bury his grandmother on Friday, then turn around and play in one of the biggest games of his life on Saturday. At a time when he would need his heart and confidence the most, one was broken and the other was shaken. Fortunately for Pete and the Michigan State Basketball team, he was able to muster up another *High Performance Maximum Xecution* shooting exhibition in the Final four semi final game against Wisconsin and he did the same in the National Championship game that Monday against Florida.

The shots he made over the weekend were not a result of passes from his teammates during those games. Instead, they were a result of the supportive passes he received earlier in the week from Tom Izzo and Mateen Cleaves. Both of them exemplified how relationship-driven leadership can be a powerful tool in providing mental and emotional support to someone in need. Their support was precisely what he needed to heal emotionally and regain his confidence before our game against Wisconsin. There is no doubt that we won the 2000 college national championship because of the relationship-driven leadership displayed by both Tom and Mateen.

Morris Peterson's shooting performances during our championship run in 2000 established him as one of the greatest shooters in the history of Michigan State Basketball.

However, in the realm of college basketball, only a select few players can truly be considered pure shooters. Morris Peterson demonstrated to the entire basketball world that he belonged to this exceptional group.

It is not uncommon for highly regarded shooters to have more good to average shooting nights than truly prolific ones. To increase their chances of having an outstanding shooting night, the best shooters in basketball understand three key principles: 1) They know how to create open opportunities for themselves. 2) They differentiate between good shots and bad shots. 3) They shoot with unwavering confidence. They believe so intently in their abilities and approach that their belief leads them to believe that every shot they take they will make.

A common characteristic of great shooters is their consistent shot preparation before releasing the basketball. This includes being on balance, having their feet set, showing their hands, and being in the ready-to-shoot position. Apart from developing the necessary fundamental skills to be a great shooter, confidence plays the most important role. Without confidence, the skill set becomes useless. Confidence is the state of mind that enhances the certainty needed to make shots. For example, the death of Pete's grandmother could have had a negative impact on his ability to shoot the ball effectively, as confidence plays a crucial role. The following two stories illustrate the significance of confidence in determining success in any aspect of life. These stories highlight the stark contrast in how confident a player or person can be in one situation compared to their lack of confidence in another situation.

I don't recall the exact year or the opposing team, but I vividly remember the events that transpired. It all took place during a time-out shortly after the start of the game. The reason for the time-out was that we fell behind by a significant margin early on. This happened because Mateen continuously passed the ball to

Pete in the corner for three-point shots during the fast breaks, but Pete missed every single one.

During the time-out, Tom immediately reprimanded both players, using his usual profane vernacular. He warned Pete, saying, "If you attempt another three-pointer, "I'll break your neck" and then directed his attention to Mateen, threatening to bench him for the remainder of the game if he passed the ball to Pete again.

Following the time-out, we transitioned to defense, successfully stopped our opponents, secured the rebound, and quickly initiated another fast break. Mateen took control of the ball, dribbling it towards our end of the court. Once again, Pete sprinted down the left lane with all his might, aiming to reach the corner for another three-point shot. Where he had previously missed the same shot three times in a row. As he arrived to the corner, Mateen passed him the ball, and Pete took the shot. This time, however, he succeeded in making the shot.

Despite receiving a harsh scolding during the previous time-out, Mateen still trusted Pete and passed him the ball. Pete didn't let Tom's comments affect him because he had confidence in his ability to make the shot, and he knew that if he was open, Mateen would pass him the ball. Tom believes in testing his players' confidence as a way to motivate them to give their best. In this particular situation, he wanted Pete to focus so that he would start making shots. No question Chief, had full confidence in Pete's shooting skills, he also understood the need to grab his attention. He wanted Pete to start making shots immediately to avoid losing the game.

The second story is quite humorous as it relates to a tale you may have probably heard as a child about Dumbo the Elephant. In case you're unfamiliar with it, here's how the story goes: Dumbo was a young circus elephant who was clumsy and had unusually large ears. Because of these traits, everyone called him Dumbo and shamelessly made fun of him. Essentially, Dumbo was mentally broken, lacking self-esteem and confidence that he would ever achieve anything significant in his entire life. However, everything changed when he befriended a clever little mouse named Timothy Q. Mouse, who gave him a feather and convinced him that its magical powers could make him capable of flying.

Pete's story is different yet similar, only in the sense that it actually happened. During Pete's junior year, he was undercut while going up for a Mateen Cleaves lob pass. When he landed, he injured his right wrist. Despite the pain, he continued playing and finished the game. Afterwards, we discovered that his wrist was broken. The injury had a significant impact on our team because Pete, our leading scorer, was a key to our string of victories at the time. However, the injury also had severe consequences for Pete's career. As a freshman, he had already taken a red shirt year, so he couldn't afford to sit out and regain that lost year. This meant that if he wanted to continue playing, he would have to do so with a cast on his wrist, which greatly limited the use of his right hand. At that time, Pete was beginning to show promise as a player, although he hadn't reached the elite or NBA level yet, he was heading in that direction. Therefore, it was crucial for him to play the remainder of the season in order to continue his development and improve his chances of being drafted into the NBA the following year.

When he received the diagnosis that his wrist would take 6 to 8 weeks to heal, he faced a life-changing decision. It was critical because if he didn't play, he would have only one more season to demonstrate his skills and prove himself as an NBA player. Secondly, he had to consider how well he could perform with a cast on his wrist, which had to be wrapped in a soft foam covering to prevent hurting others during play. The injury left him without the full use of his palm and only partial use of his fingers and thumb on his right hand. Lastly, the most important question was whether he could catch and rebound the ball effectively with his hand covered in that way.

Clearly, the odds were stacked against him, but he still made the decision to play. This decision eventually led to him becoming the first player in the history of the Big 10 to be selected to first team all Big 10 while playing as a 6th man on his team. It also played a crucial role in him being chosen as a first-round NBA draft pick the following year, ultimately earning him approximately 84 million dollars throughout his career.

How does all of this relate to the story of Dumbo the Elephant? Well, from the moment the cast was placed on Pete's hand, he immediately began playing at an exceptionally high level. It was truly amazing to watch, almost unbelievable. As coaches, we attributed his success to his heightened confidence, intensity, and focus. However, Pete firmly believed that it was the cast itself that was responsible for his outstanding performance. I'm not joking, he genuinely believed that the cast was the reason he was playing so well. In his mind, the cast became his Dumbo feather, giving him the superpower to perform at his absolute best.

When the day came for our trainer to remove the cast, Pete refused to let him do it. So, our doctor and trainer decided to gradually remove the cast bit by bit, even though his wrist was fully healed. By the last game of the regular season, there was nothing left of the cast except for a small portion that resembled a bracelet. But Pete still wouldn't allow our trainer to remove that last bit.

On game night, it is always our tradition to gather in a huddle after our team prayer before stepping onto the court to start the game. That night, after we broke the huddle, Tom asked me to join him in the training room. At the time, I had no idea why or what was happening until we entered the room. It was then that Tom informed Pete that it was time for the entire cast to be cut off his wrist. He immediately broke down in tears, while our trainer T-Mac removed the remaining portion of the cast.

Afterward, we all gathered on the floor for the announcement of the starters. As the game began, I could see the uncertainty on Pete's face as he sat on the bench, waiting for his turn to enter the game. It was clear that his confidence was shaken. When Pete finally got on the court, he passed up three open shots, providing evidence that his confidence had indeed been shaken.

Tom noticed it as well, so during the next time-out, he devised a couple of plays to create opportunities for Pete. He instructed the team to ensure Pete got open and to pass him the ball for the shot. Tom designed these plays with Antonio Smith, our best screener, in mind, knowing that Antonio could get Pete open, and Mateen, our best passer, would deliver the ball to him. Chief designed the play that way because he wanted Pete to have the best possible chance of making the shots. At the end of the timeout, I walked up to Pete, grabbed him by the arm, and said, "Shoot the ball, you're not cut that way," meaning you're not a fearful guy. Our team executed the plays just as Tom had set them up, and Pete hit two wide-open threes. After he hit the second shot, our opponents called a timeout, and Pete ran over to the bench with a big wide smile on his face because he knew he could confidently make shots without the cast (Dumbo feather) on his wrist. That night, after the game, I asked him if he had ever heard the story about Dumbo the Elephant. He said no, so right there, sitting with him in the locker room, I told him the story and how the cast was his Dumbo feather. When I was done, he burst out laughing as loud as he could.

This analogy demonstrates how the most successful shooters in the game of basketball are no different from being a shooter in the game of life. Shooters in the game of life are people who can distinguish a good (shot) opportunity from a bad (shot) opportunity. Shooters in the game of basketball have mastered the art of balancing the chances of a successful shot versus a failed one. They achieve this by establishing a strong foundation, being prepared with their feet set and hands ready, and seizing the opportunity to take a shot when it presents itself.

In basketball, simply having the ability to make shots is not enough. The first and foremost skill one must possess is the ability to get open to have opportunities for shots. However, this is not an easy task, as opponents' defenses are designed to prevent shooters from getting shots. One effective strategy against a skilled shooter is to deny them the opportunity to catch the basketball altogether. If the shooter does manage to catch the ball, their defender's job is to contest their shot. This involves extending an arm as high as possible to disrupt the flight of the ball or even block the shot. Similarly, in the game of life, shooters face similar challenges. If you want to ensure success, you must learn how to position yourself effectively and make yourself available to create shooting (opportunities) for yourself.

To create openings in the game of basketball, a shooter may strategize by having their teammates set screens for them. A screen is a technique where one teammate positions themselves as a shield, blocking the path of the opponent defending the shooter, thereby allowing the shooter to get open for a shot. Similarly, in the game of life, a comparable strategy would involve networking or seeking assistance from contacts to secure opportunities that would otherwise be inaccessible, providing you with a chance (shot) that you wouldn't typically have the opportunity to pursue.

In the game of basketball, a shot refers to the act of attempting to successfully put the ball through the basketball hoop. According to the rules, any player on the court can shoot whenever they have possession of the ball. However, not every player is considered a shooter. Among all the fundamental skills required to excel in the game of basketball, shooting is undoubtedly the most challenging skill to master. This is because what it takes to be a good shooter, let alone a great one, demands a combination of multiple skills. It requires exceptional hand-eye coordination, precise timing, and, above all, hours of repetitive practice. In reality, shooting surpasses all other skills in basketball because it is considered to be a *High Performance Maximum Xecution* skill.

One aspect of the game that is often overlooked is that many exceptional basketball players never become proficient shooters. Throughout the history of basketball, I would estimate that only about one percent of all professional players can truly be considered elite or great shooters. Mastering the art of shooting is incredibly challenging, as it involves a combination of various factors largely depending on shot distance and the type of shot being taken.

Shooting range, refers to the distance from the basket in which a player is shooting the basketball from on the court. This distance directly effects the players likelihood of successfully making shots from a specific distance. Put simply, a player may have a 60% shooting accuracy when attempting jump shots from 10 to 12 feet while facing the basket. However, if that same player attempts the same jump shot while facing the hoop from 15 feet or further away, his shooting percentage may drop by 20% or even lower.

There are so many different variables that must be measured when examining shooting proficiency. As previously mentioned, shot distance is a significant factor but so does the type of shot the player is shooting. It too can affect a player's shooting accuracy thus lowering his shooting percentages.

A good example of this would be a player who is an exceptional free throw shooter. The player's shooting percentage from the free throw line, which is located 15 feet away from the basket, is high because opponents are unable to interfere with his shot while he's shooting from the free throw line.

Now, let's compare this player to another player who has a shooting percentage of 52% from 25 feet while shooting a stand still shot. But this same player can only make 31% of his shots from 15 feet while shooting off the dribble. As you can see, there are several variables that come into play when it comes to shooting the basketball proficiently.

To explain all these variables in detail would require a great deal of time. However I thought it was important to highlight a few of the most crucial variables to give you a clearer understanding of the complexity involved in becoming an elite shooter in the game of basketball.

Similarly, becoming an elite shooter in the game of life is equally challenging. It demands consistent execution of the fundamental aspects of life's endeavors at a high-performance level. To reach such a level of execution, you must acquire proficiency in essential life skills for success, akin to those possessed by exceptional shooters in the game of basketball. The following are three necessary life skills that are crucial for personal growth and achievement:

1. EFFECTIVE COMMUNICATION: Mastering effective communication skills enables you to articulate your thoughts, understand others' perspectives, and foster meaningful connections, ultimately leading to success in various aspects of life.
2. RESILIENCE AND ADAPTABILITY: Life is full of challenges, setbacks, and unexpected changes. Developing resilience and adaptability allows you to navigate through these obstacles. Resilience helps you bounce back from failures, learn from mistakes, and maintain a positive mindset. Meanwhile, adaptability

enables you to embrace change, think creatively, and adjust your strategies when faced with new circumstances. These skills empower you to overcome adversity and thrive in spite of life shattering resistance.

3. TIME MANAGEMENT: Effective time management is essential for maximizing productivity and achieving your goals. By mastering time management skills, you can maintain the necessary focus needed to achieve your dreams and goals.

These three essential life skills—effective communication, resilience and adaptability, and time management are no different than the basic fundamental skills needed to be an elite shooter in the game of basketball. Mastering these skills you equip yourself to play the game of life successfully.

As mentioned earlier, skilled individuals in the game of life are adept at distinguishing between good and bad opportunities. This ability stems from their dedication to researching and gathering relevant information about the opportunities they pursue. Consequently, they possess the confidence to make informed decisions about the probability of success or failure associated with a particular opportunity. This readiness enables them to seize an opportunity when it arises, thanks to the solid foundation they have laid through countless hours, days, weeks, and even years of hard work. They have invested significant time and effort into acquiring the necessary knowledge to be well-prepared for capitalizing on opportunities as they arise. Consistently making free throws, whether in basketball or in life, is comparable to the skill exhibited by elite shooters.

Free throws, both in basketball and in life, are opportunities that come at no cost, and it is crucial to capitalize on them if you aim to achieve consistent success. In the game of life, I consider the following as free throw opportunities that you cannot afford to miss if you want to be successful:1) Make the most of educational opportunities by fully committing yourself to self-improvement. With dedication to the learning process, you will discover the most effective ways for you to absorb information. Understanding your most productive learning methods is paramount during your school years, as it will significantly enhance your ability to grasp future learning opportunities. Personally, I can speak from experience on the importance of investing effort into self-education. During high school, I neglected to prioritize my educational growth. I received warnings from two of my closest friends, Keith Simons and Tony Ogletree. They both advised me to take college prep classes in order to prepare for college. However, I made the decision to enroll in general curriculum classes throughout high school. As a consequence, I found myself unprepared for the required SAT examination and struggled to succeed in college. One thing I never shared with anyone, not even my closest friends, was that my primary reason for avoiding college prep classes was my poor reading ability. While my reading comprehension was fairly good, I was an extremely slow reader. I believed that I wouldn't be able to keep up with the pace of college prep classes due to this issue. Looking back, if I had been mature enough to address my reading problem at the time, I am confident that the teachers at my high school would have assisted me in overcoming this obstacle. I am also certain that the teachers who taught the college prep classes would have dedicated extra time to help me succeed in their courses.

Eventually, my lack of education caught up with me when I failed to achieve the minimum required SAT score to receive a basketball scholarship to Michigan State University. It was a shameful moment because I had good grades, but I had neglected my studies in high school, particularly in properly educating myself. As a result, my dream of playing basketball at Michigan State was shattered. After taking the SAT exam for the last time and failing to achieve the necessary score, I decided to call Gus Ganakas, who was the head basketball coach at Michigan State at that time. In an attempt to hide my disappointment, I lied to him about why I wanted to go to Northern Michigan University instead of Michigan State. After hanging up the phone, I sat in my basement, tears streaming down my face, terrified that I wouldn't be able to attend college anywhere. I felt both embarrassed and afraid to discuss my situation with anyone. Eventually, I gathered the courage to call Lloyd Carr, one of my high school football coaches. Looking back, I truly believe that phone call changed the trajectory of my life. When I explained what had happened to Coach Carr, he immediately suggested that I consider attending Northern Michigan University (NMU). His reason for suggesting that I do so was that I could receive a basketball scholarship to play in Division II without needing the required SAT test score for Division I basketball at Michigan State.

Although Northern Michigan wasn't my first choice, it turned out to be the best thing that could have happened to me in the long run for my career as a college basketball coach. I firmly believe that all the positive experiences I've had as a basketball coach wouldn't have occurred if I hadn't attended NMU. I would have never formed a lifelong relationship with Chief (Tom Izzo) and probably wouldn't have had the opportunity to coach college basketball. I'm also extremely grateful to a learning specialist at NMU named Sally Satterfield, who helped me develop the fundamental reading and writing skills necessary to succeed in college.

Secondly, it is crucial for you to fully capitalize on college scholarships, grants, or any other types of funding available to assist you in pursuing higher education, whether it be college, trade school, or technical training. These opportunities will enable you to acquire the necessary knowledge and skills required to compete effectively in the job market. In the event that you are not fortunate enough to receive a scholarship, explore alternative avenues such as grants, loans, or even working to finance your education. It is important to recognize that a degree not only reflects your intelligence but also speaks to your character. It signifies that you are a responsible and disciplined individual who is committed to completing tasks.

Thirdly, it is essential to learn from the experiences of successful individuals. Engage in activities such as reading books, listening to podcasts, and, whenever possible, engaging in face-to-face conversations with accomplished individuals who are willing to share their wisdom. By studying their journeys and insights, you can gain valuable knowledge and guidance to apply to your own path to success. For example, if your goal is to excel as a public speaker, it would be beneficial for you to invest time in studying other accomplished speakers like Barack Obama, ET Eric Thomas, or Tony Robbins. By analyzing their speeches and observing their mannerisms, you can learn valuable techniques just as you would by studying how skilled basketball players perform and applying their strategies to your own game.

When I made the decision to become a high school basketball coach, I made a concerted effort to attend as many coaching clinics as possible. My objective was to acquire the necessary knowledge and skills to effectively prepare a team. To achieve this, I eagerly attended practices at various high schools, colleges, and even professional basketball teams. At that time, I focused my studies on two coaches in particular: Chuck Daley, the former head coach of the back-to-back Detroit Piston NBA championship teams during the legendary Bad Boys Era of professional basketball. The other coach was Perry Watson. During that time, he had the best high school program in the state of Michigan and eventually built one of the top high school programs in the country. Later, he became an assistant coach at the University of Michigan during the famous Fab 5 era. After a brief period there, he went on to become the winningest coach in the history of University of Detroit basketball.

To this day, I am grateful to Perry for the time he spent mentoring me, without any expectations in return. Trust me, the value of mentorship is priceless. Therefore, I suggest you find a mentor who can teach you what you need to learn and how to successfully implement the knowledge you have acquired. One of the most helpful things I have learned over the years is that most successful people don't try to reinvent the wheel. More often, they take the blueprint of another successful person and use it as a template to devise their own plan for success. Tom Izzo did this when he became the head coach at Michigan State. He wisely took Jud Heathcote's system and made adjustments to fit the style he wanted his teams to play. This style of play has earned him a place in the National Basketball Hall of fame. My ultimate recommendation is to seize every opportunity to volunteer, as community service and volunteer work frequently lead to future opportunities that may not otherwise arise. Additionally, the personal rewards derived from engaging in volunteer work are truly invaluable.

Years ago, my wife Cynthia and I became foster parents to children who had been neglected by mothers struggling with addiction during the country's crack cocaine epidemic. I vividly recall the first two children we took in; Donald, an infant at the time, and his sister Shatara, who was around two or three years old. They had both been abandoned by their mother for approximately ten days, according to the social services professionals.

Unfortunately, their tragic circumstances had taken a toll on them, both physically and mentally. Shatara, for instance, had developed a habit of rummaging through our garbage can in search of food. It was a behavior she likely acquired during her time of abandonment. To manage her care, my oldest son Quentin and I took charge, while my wife Cynthia and daughter Simone focused on attending to Donald, who had his own serious health issues and required round-the-clock care.

During one particular day of caring for Shatara, Quentin and I found ourselves repeatedly pulling her away from the garbage can as she persistently tried to eat from it. Even though we made sure to provide her with food each time, she continued with her behavior. It had reached a point where I was completely frustrated and unsure of what to do about a habit that was harming her health. Realizing that I had no practical solutions, I decided to pray and ask the Lord for guidance in breaking her habit. Just as I finished my prayer, I looked up and saw my son giving her something from the refrigerator. It was in that moment that the solution became clear to me. I immediately instructed Quentin to leave the refrigerator door open and allow her to continue taking whatever she wanted until she was so full that she couldn't eat anymore. That day, my prayer was answered, as we never had any further trouble with her rummaging through the garbage for food.

However, her brother Donald presented a different challenge. Being an infant, he couldn't take care of himself like his sister did when they were abandoned and had to resort to eating from the garbage can. Sadly, all he could do was cry and hope that someone would come to feed him. Unfortunately, his constant crying led to a health issue that made it difficult for us to nurse him back to health. The problem arose from his weak stomach muscles, which were a result of constant crying and sucking without receiving any nourishment—only air. As a consequence, he was unable to independently consume formula from a bottle like a typical infant would. We decided to consult our pediatrician for guidance on how to address this issue. Our pediatrician explained to us that when a baby goes for prolonged periods without being fed, their body instinctively responds by involuntarily attempting to suck in nourishment. This involuntary sucking response persists until the stomach muscles weaken to the point where they can no longer suck effectively. Unfortunately, this was precisely what had happened to Donald, compounded by the fact that he was also born addicted to crack cocaine. The pediatrician informed us that there were limited medical options available to address the feeding problem. Instead, my wife and daughter initially feed him using a small spoon and gradually transition to a tiny squeeze bottle that resembles a toy bottle used for doll play as he grew stronger.

After the doctor's visit, my wife and daughter embarked on the tireless task of restoring Donald's health. They diligently fed him several times a day and night, as he could only consume small amounts of food during each feeding. They also provided manual assistance with his bowel movements, as he lacked the abdominal strength to do it himself. Additionally, due to his status as a crack baby, they constantly monitored him for withdrawal symptoms. They took turns bathing him three or four times a day, as his body emitted a foul odor and his skin resembled fish scales from head to toe. As they tenderly rubbed and scrubbed his tiny body, our bathtub would become filled with the residue they washed off him, resembling a sewage ditch. Initially, his skin was very dark, but under their care, it gradually lightened by two shades.

Even though many years have passed, I still feel immensely proud of my wife and daughter whenever I think about what they did for a child who was not related to us. Their care and unwavering kindness in restoring Donald's health, without seeking recognition or reward, is a testament to their compassionate and selfless Christ like nature. All highly skilled individuals in the game of life understand that volunteering and possessing an empathetic heart is akin to consistently scoring three-pointers without ever missing. Every act of kindness towards others is equivalent to making a game-winning shot each and every time.

Fundamental #4 Rebounding

Adreian (AP) Payne Tom (Chief) Izzo

Adreian Payne, well before his Michigan State playing days, embodied the essence of a rebounder, not only in basketball but also in life. Tragically, at the tender age of thirteen, he had to rebound from the death of his mother, Gloria, who took her last breath in his arms.

One day, unexpectedly, Adreian walked into my office and sat down directly across from me in total silence. I immediately sensed that something serious was weighing on his mind. Whenever Adreian wanted to discuss something, he would enter my office silently, just as he did that day, which was uncharacteristic for this usually talkative young man. Recognizing the seriousness of his demeanor, I initiated a conversation without further delay, knowing he was a young man grappling with deep-seated emotional trauma.

Gloria's death haunted Adreian at times, and when it did, he often needed to vent to alleviate the undeserved hurt and guilt he carried. On this particular day, I closed my office door and asked him, "Peezy, what's troubling you?" He began to recount his story, "OG, she asked me, 'Adreian, go get my inhaler.' I searched everywhere upstairs but couldn't find it. When I returned, she was lying on the kitchen floor. I didn't know what to do, so I held her in my arms and told her I looked everywhere but couldn't find it. Then, she died in my arms." After he finished speaking, we both sat in silence, heads down. He then looked me straight in the eye, and I reassured him, "It's ain't your fault, man.

Adreian was an individual with a big heart, as evidenced by his affection for small children. His ability to bring smiles to the faces of hospitalized children was unmatched. However, he was not always an easy teammate or player to coach. I have always believed that his inability to overcome the guilt of his mother's death was due to a lack of appropriate help early on, which could have provided closure. I also believe that the absence of this support impeded his social development. Despite this, Adreian was the type of person who could have a confrontation with someone and then, an hour later, be generous enough to give them the shirt off his back.

A mere six years after his mother's death, he was forced to grapple with another unexpected loss: his beloved grandmother, Mary Lewis. The circumstances of her passing were ironically poignant. Just hours before her death, he had visited her home to bid farewell before returning to East Lansing for his sophomore year at Michigan State. He recounted to me that on the day of her death, in an unusual act, his grandmother stood in the doorway, watching him drive away as if it were their final goodbye. This struck him as strange because it was something she had never done before. He recalled that as he drove down the street, he could still see her in his rear-view mirror, standing in the doorway. As he turned the corner, she stepped onto the porch and waved at him again, as if it were her last chance to bid him farewell. Tragically, his intuition proved correct when he received news of her passing later that night from his brother.

As if life hadn't presented him with enough trials, he was then faced with the death of an eight-year-old cancer patient named Lacey Holsworth, endearingly known as Princess Lacey. He had developed a unique private bond with her during his freshman year, which only became public knowledge in his senior year. Lacey's death came as he was reeling from one of the toughest losses of his college career. She passed away just after our loss to Connecticut in the Elite 8 round of the 2014 NCAA tournament. Winning that game would have propelled the team to the 2014 Final Four, with a shot at the national championship. Adding to the sting of defeat, this loss made him part of the first group of seniors to play four years under coach Tom Izzo without ever reaching the Final Four. However, in the midst of these challenging times, he found a reason to celebrate. He was selected as the 15th player in the 2014 NBA draft, making him the first pick for the Atlanta Hawks.

When we first recruited Adreian, Coach Tom Izzo was skeptical, largely due to well-known academic issues. Adreian and I had similar struggles, particularly with reading. Yet, despite these obstacles, he persevered, marking one of the most extraordinary times in his life. While he certainly wasn't lacking in intellectual capacity, he was like so many urban Black children who are the unfortunate victims of inadequate school systems.

Dwayne Stephens and I loved AP, but Tom might not have ever agreed to take Adreian on board if it hadn't been for a particular incident. Initially unsettling to Tom, this incident ultimately swayed his decision. The first time Tom got a chance to watch AP play, he was immediately dismissive, thinking AP was irresponsible - especially since he arrived, rushing through the gym to get dressed, just two minutes before the game started. In Tom's mind, coupled with AP's academic issues, this was another red flag.

Whenever Tom or any other member of our staff attends a player's game, we make sure to arrive early. We observe not just the warm-up routine, but crucially, the interaction between the player, his teammates, and his coaches. With less than five minutes left in the warm-up and Adreian nowhere to be found, Tom, frustrated, called me and Dwayne Stephens. We had encouraged him to watch AP despite his initial reluctance to recruit him. However, in the middle of our conversation, Adreian appeared, dashing through the gym. Before hanging up, Tom expressed his disappointment, "Why would you and DJ suggest recruiting a kid who is so disrespectful that he thinks he can arrive late to a game, especially knowing I was coming to watch him play?"

Earlier that afternoon, Tom met separately with Adreian and Dr. Gates, the superintendent of Jefferson Township schools, in his office. That's why he was so frustrated, and justifiably so. The term 'schools' wasn't entirely fitting for AP's school district, as there was only one building that accommodated every student in the entire district from kindergarten to 12th grade. The only other structure was the administration office, located across the parking lot from the school.

It was crucial that Tom met with Dr. Gates, as he had a special interest in Adreian, and we knew he would have significant influence when it came time for AP to decide his schooling. During their conversation, Tom felt that Dr. Gates was candid about Adreian, sharing both his strengths and weaknesses. In the same conversation, Dr. Gates assured Tom that if he had the chance to coach AP, he would never have to question his character.

That night, Tom formed the belief that Dr. Gates was a BS guy, attempting to protect a problematic player, due to AP's tardiness for the game. In the afternoon, although Dr. Gates discussed various matters with Tom regarding AP, he neglected to mention that he was AP's math tutor. Tom only discovered this fact after the game that night, when Adreian's coaches, Mark Parker and Art Winston, explained it to him. They revealed that Dr. Gates was extremely strict about discipline and accountability, and during tutorial sessions, AP was not allowed to leave Dr. Gates' office until they had accomplished their objectives. This meant that AP sometimes had to miss practice or a game if he didn't complete the obligations set for him during his tutorial with Dr. Gates.

Art and Mark's explanation delighted Tom because it confirmed that Adreian possessed the qualities of players whom he had transformed into successful student athletes and outstanding players.

Later, we learned that Tom was the only college head coach with whom Dr. Gates had spent significant time during Adreian's recruitment process. Mark Parker and Art Winston informed us that Dr. Gates had been willing to invest time with Tom because he had thoroughly researched every school that was interested in Adreian. Dr. Gates was already aware of our graduation rate and our track record of supporting academically challenged students, leading him to believe that we would prioritize Adreian's academic success. It was refreshing to learn that Adreian was recruited based on our academic success rather than our basketball achievements, which is how it should be. As soon as Adreian arrived on campus, we began ensuring his academic success, just as Dr. Gates had predicted. We promptly assigned him to Gretchen Paige, who was not only the best learning specialist on campus at the time but also, in Tom's and my opinion, the best we've ever had at MSU. Gretchen took a personal interest in Adreian, not only in his academics but also in his overall growth as a young man. Thanks to her hard work and dedication to Adreian's academic success, he was able to graduate from Michigan State with a degree. Despite the constant challenges he faced, Adreian's ability to rebound from those circumstances has always been his unique strength, allowing him to achieve things in life that many of his critics believed were impossible for him. What's most interesting about Adreian is that his most significant attribute as a basketball player was his ability to rebound. This same skill enabled him to overcome multiple tragic incidents in the game of life.

Unfortunately, on May 9th, 2022, Adreian was tragically shot and killed while trying to help a friend of his girlfriend who was in a violent and toxic relationship with her boyfriend. As I understand it, Adreian's girlfriend called him, asking for his help to pick her up so they could go to her friend's house. The friend wanted to leave her house with her kids, but her boyfriend was preventing them from leaving. However, because they lived far apart, Adreian told his girlfriend that he would meet her at the friend's house.

When Adreian arrived at the house, the boyfriend and his father approached him in the front yard. As soon as he parked his car, they immediately confronted him, likely feeling intimidated by his size. The father then threatened to retrieve his gun from inside the house. Both the father and the son went into the house, retrieved the gun, and when they returned, the son shot Adreian in the chest, instantly killing him.

It's important to note that Adreian was not a stranger to the boyfriend. In fact, he, his girlfriend, the boyfriend, and the boyfriend's girlfriend had been on several double dates together. He must have been fully aware that Adreian had no intention of causing harm to them or his girlfriend. It has been said that Adreian and his girlfriend had visited the house on multiple occasions in the past to intervene during other instances of violent disputes between the couple. It doesn't make sense why the boyfriend would kill him. I believe that the boyfriend's father encouraged him to kill Adreian, even though he knew very well that Adreian posed no real threat to him.

Now, the next statement I'm about to make regarding Adreian's death may upset many people. If it does, I genuinely don't care because the level of gun violence in our country is shockingly out of control. This is primarily due to the lack of necessary leadership to implement proper and safe gun laws. Adreian's death is not solely the fault of the person who pulled the trigger, but it is also the responsibility of every politician in our country who opposes stricter gun laws. Adreian, may you rest in peace, even though I know it will be difficult for you and all those who have tragically lost their lives to gun violence.

A rebound in the game of basketball happens when a player retrieves the ball after another player's missed shot, or sometimes when the rebounder retrieves his own missed shot. If the rebounder retrieves his own missed shot or a teammate's, it's counted as an offensive rebound. However, if he retrieves an opponent's missed shot, it's counted as a defensive rebound.

The top rebounders possess what's known as a "nose for the ball," meaning they have a natural ability to anticipate where the ball will come off the rim and position themselves accordingly to grab it. These instinctive rebounders also excel in timing, enabling them to rebound the ball above the rim or outside their immediate playing area, which is termed a "range rebound." Their well-honed timing also allows them to secure "clean rebounds," where no opposing player challenges them for the ball.

High-level rebounders adopt a consistent mindset whenever a shot is taken, assuming that every shot will be missed. Consequently, they always position themselves to transform a missed shot into a positive outcome, often creating another scoring opportunity for their team.

Comparatively, the best rebounders in the game of life share similar traits with rebounders in the game of basketball. When faced with a failed opportunity, life's rebounders quickly recover and move forward. They understand that a missed chance is simply another opportunity to succeed in the future. Life's rebounders are individuals who are not afraid to take risks and pursue their dreams, knowing that the potential rewards of success outweigh the risks of failure. They are fearless because they have prepared themselves to bounce back if their current pursuit doesn't work out. They already have a plan in mind for how, when, and where their next opportunity for success will arise. Consequently, they can confidently move on after a setback because they have diligently researched and rebounded to another opportunity before the missed chance occurs.

The 1997-98 season was a critical time for Tom Izzo, our staff (which included Tom Crean, Stan Heath, and myself), and the future success of the Michigan State Basketball program as we know it today. It was Chief's (Tom Izzo's) third year as head coach, and we were under immense pressure to achieve significant victories. Failure to do so would have put our jobs at risk by the end of the season.

I vividly recall a particular incident during that season when Tom and I were sitting in his car in the Breslin Center tunnel, listening to a radio show discussing the possibility of us being fired. This conversation took place after we had suffered three losses out of four games against mid-level teams, which were considered bad defeats for a high-profile basketball program. As we sat there, Tom's mother called, having heard the same radio show, expressing her distress and concern that he might lose his job. I witnessed tears streaming down Tom's face as he tried to reassure her that everything would be alright. After he finished the call, I spoke up and said, "Chief, they ain't firing us, they ain't running us out. If we leave, it will be on our own, not because they ran us out. The rest of our staff and I will help you improve our players immediately."

However, we faced the challenge of already being in the midst of the season, and the usual practice protocol discouraged excessive training. But we had no choice but to do it anyway. The following morning, our staff collectively made the decision to intensify our efforts by doubling or even tripling our workouts because we recognized the urgency to rapidly improve our team's performance.

We ended up in this situation because the past two previous seasons were mediocre at best. In the 1995-96 season, we had an overall record of 16-16, finished 7th in the Big Ten, and lost in the 2nd round of the NIT. The 1996-97 season was slightly better, with a record of 17-12, tied for 6th in the Big Ten, but we again lost in the 2nd round of the NIT. These two consecutive mediocre seasons undoubtedly presented challenging times for our young and ambitious staff as we navigated the competitive world of college basketball, trying to keep our jobs.

Despite the difficulties, these tough times brought us closer together as a staff. As a matter of fact, if need be, I can reach out to any member of that staff, and they would be there for me without hesitation. In the world of sports, you often hear stories about players who play for each other. However, in our case, we were a group of coaches who were coaching for one another. Each one of us understood that the fate of our families, careers, and legacies hung in the balance if we didn't achieve immediate success. This understanding fostered a culture among our staff that demanded we never let each other down. We were fully aware that this was our moment, and we had to rely on one another to make it happen. It may sound crazy, but looking back, I wouldn't trade that experience for anything because I didn't just go through it, I grew through it.

Now, the unanswered question was, "What would be our winning strategy?" In other words, what was the key factor that would lead us to victory in the majority of our remaining games this season? This is where Tom Izzo's brilliance comes into play as a coach. He recognized that we needed to score points to win games, but we struggled with shooting. This prompted him to find a way to turn our weakness into a strength. And he found the answer: rebounding.

His strategy had two main components. First, we would ensure that our opponents never got more than one shot attempt on each of their possessions. Every game, our goal was to prevent our opponents from getting second or third shot attempts. This put tremendous pressure on them to make over 50% of their shots in order to beat us, which is nearly impossible if they only have one shot attempt per possession. Furthermore, this strategy limited the number of points our opponents could score against us in a game.

Second, our team would do to our opponents what we were determined not to let happen to us – we would secure second, third, and sometimes even fourth shot attempts. We would capitalize on offensive rebounds and give ourselves extra scoring opportunities.

By focusing on these two aspects – preventing second chances for our opponents and generating additional scoring opportunities for ourselves – we were able to transform our shooting disadvantage into an advantage. This strategic approach not only increased our chances of winning games, but it also showcased Tom Izzo's coaching ingenuity.

To execute our strategy, we employed a unique approach during that era of basketball. Whenever we attempted a shot, we would send four players to aggressively rebound the ball. This went against conventional thinking at the time, which advocated always sending two players back on defense to prevent easy baskets by the opponent in transition. However, our approach was tailored to our team's strengths and weaknesses. Since we didn't make many shots, our missed shot attempts became our best opportunity to score. Our players embraced the challenge of rebounding, turning missed shots into put-backs for scores. A put-back is a lay-up shot scored as close to the basket as possible by the player who rebounds the ball after a missed shot. Chief's decision to make rebounding the cornerstone of our playing style and fearlessly implement a strategy around it was undoubtedly a stroke of genius.

A stroke of genius that led to us winning the 1997-98 *national rebounding title* by a +15 *rebounding margin* which is the number of *rebounds* we out *rebounded* our opponents in every game.

Which is an astounding number and is currently still the record for *rebounding margin* today.

Because of that accomplishment *rebounding and toughness* became a *national brand* for the Michigan State basketball program.

Good coaches understand their team's problems, but great coaches not only identify those problems but also develop solutions for them. Chief (Tom Izzo) is a Hall of Fame coach because he consistently demonstrates his ability to find solutions to his team's problems, particularly how he used rebounding to establish a culture of high performance and maximum execution. He convinced his team to view missed shots as opportunities rather than failures. His teams quickly turned their scoring failures into chances for immediate short-term success by rebounding over 50% of their missed shots and converting them into easy baskets. This strategic focus on rebounding not only ensured their short-term success but also boosted their confidence to play with a relentless determination never witnessed before in college basketball.

In addition, Chief understood that the success his team gained from rebounding the ball would also translate into a culture of confidence and swagger that would eventually become the brand of the Michigan State basketball program. It became a culture of relentless rebounding and toughness that has served as the blueprint for 25 years of unprecedented championship basketball. The ability to bounce back, recover, or, better put, rebound from failure is not something exclusive to Tom Izzo, Adreian Payne, or the Michigan State basketball program.

Please hear me when I tell you that if an ordinary guy from Iron Mountain, Michigan named Tom Izzo can accomplish extraordinary things, you can too. *However, you must be willing to do things at a High Performance Maximum Xecution level all the time*. Both Tom and Adreian are great examples of what you can achieve, regardless of your ambitions in life, by consistently rebounding from the hardships and heartaches of failure.

In 2018 Chief (Tom Izzo) had to rebound from being unjustifiable casted into the Larry Nassar molestation scandal. Currently Larry Nassar is serving a 40 to 175 year prison sentence for the sexual assault of young women and children while he was the osteopathic physician for the US Olympic gymnastics team and Michigan State university. The scrutiny cut so deeply into the very core of Tom's soul that he literally had difficulty showing his face publicly.

The situation disheartened him so much that, for the first time in his career, he actually contemplated leaving his beloved Michigan State University for the NBA or some other college basketball program. To this day, he feels that his integrity was unfairly damaged to the point where it cannot be restored to what it once was prior to Larry Nassar's unforgivable, horrific crimes. To add insult to injury, he felt abandoned by those in the media and the Lansing community at large whom he thought were sincere friends and associates throughout his time at Michigan State. He couldn't believe how so many of them openly questioned his character, integrity, and reputation for always doing things the right way, despite knowing him for nearly all of his adult life. People whom he always thought would stand up as character witnesses to his high degree of integrity, many of whom have known him upfront and personally for a number of years, elected not to take a stand in his defense. Unfortunately, I believe that many of them don't realize that their relationship with him has been permanently damaged. He has continued to harbor this hurt because of how it not only hurt him but even more so how the scrutiny damaged his family, the university, and our players.

The majority of people don't realize how much a distraction like the Larry Nassar situation can negatively affect a team.

Remember, all of this took place in the middle of one of the best seasons in Michigan State basketball history. Once the scrutiny was cast on Chief, it was also cast onto our players. As the scrutiny continued to mount, our team began to struggle to win games. This happened because our guys put undue pressure on themselves to win, thinking that they had to win to keep Tom and our staff from being fired.

That year, we ended the season with a 30-5 record and a Big 10 regular-season championship. Although our team handled the pressure the best they could throughout the majority of the season, by the end of the season, the pressure finally got to them and we lost our last two games. The first loss was to Michigan in the second round of the Big 10 tournament, and the second loss was to Syracuse in the second round of the NCAA tournament. In both games, we couldn't manage to make a shot after going through the entire season as one of the top shooting teams in college basketball from both two-point and three-point range. That year, the pressure from the Larry Nassar scandal brought a disappointing end to what was shaping up to be a Final Four, possibly national championship season.

Following our defeat to Syracuse, we gathered in the locker room with conflicting emotions: sorrow and relief. We mourned the missed opportunities that could have been achieved under normal conditions, while simultaneously feeling relieved to escape the intense scrutiny imposed on us by our fans, the public, and especially the media.

Fortunately, we have all managed to recover from an unjustifiable situation that was unrelated to Tom or our basketball program. None of our players had any acquaintance with Larry Nassar. During my entire tenure at MSU, I rarely encountered him in our facility, maybe only three or four times. Nevertheless, life presents such situations occasionally, emphasizing the importance of being able *rebound*.

The following OG'ism is a proactive approach to life that will minimize the number of times you'll have to unnecessarily experience rebounding from failure. I'm not saying that you won't ever experience hardship, heartache, and failure if you adhere to my OG'ism. However, you can minimize unnecessary failure by developing this one simple habit: "Always try to defeat the spirit of defeat before it defeats you!"

In essence, what I'm saying to you is to take inventory of the things that can cause defeat in your life. Then, take action to address them before they have a chance to destroy your opportunities for success. If you want to find out exactly what causes you to be defeated, you must be willing to look in the mirror and ask yourself, "What am I doing wrong? What is the one thing I'm doing wrong that I could fix but won't fix, that I can fix if I would?" Then, think about it, and you'll get the answer. But it won't always be the answer you want, but it will be the necessary one.

Fundamental #5 Playing with Speed and Quickness

Steve Smith

Great players know how to play the game of basketball with speed and quickness while staying under control. They understand the value of being quick but not hurried, the importance of changing speeds, and the significance of patience. Similarly, great individuals in the game of life exhibit these qualities. While they aspire to achieve success as quickly as possible, they recognize that hastiness and a lack of patience can be critical detours on the road to success.

Today's technology, particularly social media, allows us immediate access to information, fostering a culture of instant gratification that often overlooks the process. As a result, we have created an entire society that views success as something that can be achieved instantaneously. It's a common belief among many people today that the process is an unnecessary step in their pursuit of success.

I started my coaching career in Belleville, Michigan, as a 30-year-old high school JV basketball coach. Up until that point, I had no prior coaching experience, except for the volunteer work I did with Tom Izzo during his first job as a head coach at Ishpeming High School. After that, my only other coaching experience was at Detroit Cody High School with Robert Menefee and William Eddie, one of my teammates from my playing days at Northern Michigan University.

Today, it's hard to believe that back in college I had no ambition of becoming a basketball coach. In May of 1977, I graduated with a Bachelor of Science in Physical Education and Recreation but decided not to return the following fall to complete my Teacher's Certification.

"That was a decision that turned out to be a significant mistake, yet it was a mistake that taught me the value of patience. At the time, potential regrets didn't concern me; I was eager to own my own business, strike it rich, and transition from rags to riches overnight. However, fate had other plans, and my dreams of rapid wealth never materialized. Reflecting on it now, several reasons contributed to this failed dream. The main one was that I tried to achieve something outside of what I believe God had intended for my life.

Throughout my life, I've always sensed my purpose would eventually revolve around teaching. I didn't always want to accept this calling, but I knew it was mine, yet I still denied it. I didn't know then what type of teacher I was supposed to be, but my intuition urged me: teach. I didn't know whether I was meant to be a school teacher, a teacher of God's word (a preacher), or a sports teacher (a coach).

74

Part of this understanding came from my grandmother, Bessie Seed. As a child, I would often overhear her telling family and friends about my early passion for teaching. Deep down, I knew the path intended for me. However, I chose not to pursue the destiny I believed God had set for me. Instead, right out of college, I took a position with a landscaping company for which I had worked as a young kid. It was owned by a family friend named Wesley Charles.

I admired Wesley. He was a successful, wealthy, young African American businessman who had built his business literally from scratch seemingly overnight. In my mind, the opportunity to work for Wesley offered everything I needed to realize my dream, as he had done, rapidly transitioning from rags to riches without considering the process necessary to fulfill my ambition.

All that occupied my mind at that time was making money—and lots of it—as quickly as possible. I didn't realize then that time was actually the key to running a successful business and generating wealth. Back then, even if I had understood the concept that "time is money," I wouldn't have been willing to accept it because I was in such a rush. This mistake, however, taught me a very valuable lesson: patience is a virtue, a principle applicable to all aspects of life."

Steve Smith is a man I hold in high regard because of his generous spirit. When most people think of Steve Smith, they envision the NBA All-Star, Olympic Gold Medalist, and NBA World Champion. They remember him as a two-time consensus All-American and the 1989 Big 10 Conference Champion. His accolades as a college player at Michigan State are just as impressive as his achievements as an NBA player. Smith was the 5th player selected overall out of the 30 first-round picks by the Miami Heat in the 1991 NBA draft.

While Steve's basketball accomplishments are well-recognized, his most admirable trait—his philanthropy—has not been equally acknowledged. His charitable contributions include a $3 million gift to build a state-of-the-art academic center for student-athletes at Michigan State, named after his mother, Clara Bell Smith. He also established the Steve Smith Scholarship for Academic Achievement, which offers a four-year scholarship to Michigan State for inner-city youth every year. He continues to donate generously to this scholarship fund to ensure it remains well-financed. These acts are just a few examples of Smith's many charitable contributions, which are clear evidence of his giving heart.

Steve was an extraordinary athlete, but it wasn't just his athleticism that made him an exceptional basketball player—it was his intelligence. His keen understanding of the game was so respected that, immediately after his playing career ended, the NBA and several major television networks sought him out as an analytical broadcasting expert for both NBA and college basketball games. Like most elite players, Smith used his innate intelligence and understanding of the game to play efficiently and effectively. He recognized that basketball is a game of rhythm and utilized this knowledge, along with his court awareness, to master controlling the games rhythm and the pace at which he played. Smith was adept at keeping his opponents off balance by altering the tempo and speed of his game, thereby preventing them from being able to stop him from scoring.

Steve Smith is the perfect embodiment, both on and off the court, of the legendary coach John Wooden's philosophy: "Be Quick, But Don't Hurry." Successful individuals, such as Steve Smith, understand the importance of being quick but not hasty, as it relates to life. People who are always in a hurry tend to make mistakes because their impatience puts them in a state of mind that negatively affects their judgment, their ability to make clear decisions, and ultimately any chance they would have to execute at a high-performance maximum Xecution level. While it's important to avoid being in a hurry, there are times in your efforts to succeed where speed and quickness must be employed to seize a particular opportunity.

In basketball, players with exceptional speed and the intelligence to effectively apply it are usually the most dominant. An example of this can be seen when a basketball player goes from zero to top speed in just two or three steps, which is a demonstration of quickness. In contrast, a player's ability to maintain top speed on steps four, five, and six, and then move even faster on steps seven, eight, nine, and ten, is considered speed. A common example of speed in basketball is when a player dribbles the ball from one end of the court to the other and scores a basket before anyone on the opposing team can stop them. The best players understand that speed and quickness are selective and should only be used intentionally, not as a last resort. When used properly, speed and quickness can provide an advantage in basketball or in life. However, when they are not employed properly, they can result in a disadvantage.

Consider a scenario where a player uses his speed and quickness to dribble the length of the court and score a basket. However, this time, his opponents are already back, defending the basket, making it impossible for him to dribble all the way to the basket and score. Despite the other team's defense being set up to stop him, he is still determined to use his speed to dribble the full length of the court and score. As a result of his poor judgment, he runs head-on into one of the opponents who is protecting the basket. The play ends badly with a foul on him, resulting in a turnover and a lost opportunity for his team to score. Possession of the ball goes back to the other team. In this instance, the player's eagerness to score caused him to hurry, leading to the misuse of his speed and quickness, which ended in disaster. Speed and quickness, if not used intelligently, can significantly diminish your chances for success in both basketball and life.

The appropriate use of speed and quickness holds dynamic similarities in both life and basketball, which is why it's possible to draw relatable analogies between the two that can be easily understood. The following analogy supports my earlier point.

I have personally witnessed and experienced what happens when long-awaited, once-in-a-lifetime opportunities suddenly appear. Most of the time, they show up unexpectedly, without warning, and with a sense of urgency. When opportunities materialize abruptly, it often means that to seize them, you may need to act swiftly. The Bible tells us that David ran to do battle with Goliath. He did this because he knew that his moment of glory was imminent, but he also knew that any procrastination could cost him this opportunity.

Similarly, when you're faced with a chance to fulfill a lifetime goal or dream, you may be required to pursue it with both speed and quickness. This is because the successful realization of your goal, dream, or a long-awaited opportunity could hinge on your ability to meet specific deadlines or quotas, and simultaneously deliver what is needed at a high-performance maximum Xecution level. However, be vigilant not to let the pressure to seize your opportunities lead you into panic or tempt you to hurry. Trust me when I tell you, as I previously mentioned, that there will come a day when your dream opportunity will depend on your ability to deliver at a high-performance maximum Xecution level as soon as possible to make your dream come true. Keep in mind, however, that even though you may need to move fast, remember to be quick but don't hurry. As I stated earlier in this chapter, a common characteristic among all successful individuals (or players) is that they know how to navigate the game of life (or basketball) with speed and quickness, without hurry.

Fundamental #6 Toughness

Andre (Dre) Hutson Michael (Ray) Garland

Tom Izzo has built a college basketball dynasty at Michigan State on the premise that his teams would be the *toughest* in college basketball. In his third season at the helm, he coined the phrase "PP-TPW," which means "*players play, tough players win.*" Hence, the *toughness* mentality that has become the *brand* for Michigan State basketball as we know it today.

Tom vehemently believes that toughness is the true indicator of a person's will to succeed in the game of life. I, too, believe that mentally tough individuals are able to endure difficult times throughout their lives. They firmly believe that tough times are temporary, but tough people endure. Tough individuals possess a higher pain threshold, enabling them to confidently face hardships. However, I also acknowledge that discipline and determination contribute to the development of mental and physical toughness.

During my time at Michigan State, I have observed Chief transform individuals who were not mentally or physically tough into resilient players. He molds them into "beasts" by teaching them how to remain relentless in the face of adversity. Chief excels at motivating his players and helping them harness their toughness to secure victories. He strongly believes that a player's confidence is directly linked to their toughness.

In essence, Tom believes that if a player thinks he is tough, he will be tough. Chief instills toughness in his players by consistently putting them into situations that challenge their mental and physical strength daily. During the early days of the program, we put our players through a drill we call "WAR." Back then, we played three segments of our WAR game for ten to fifteen minutes during practice every day. We even played it before a few of our games in those days.

WAR is simply a 5-on-5 rebounding drill that becomes highly competitive due to the physical contact. Aside from excessive force, like attempting to take a player's head off, everything is permitted. The objective of the drill is to foster a mentality of toughness in our players so they understand they can play physically without getting injured. Once this mentality is established, they're not afraid to dive for loose balls or fight for rebounds in a crowd.

Every year, numerous basketball coaches at all levels visit our practice to understand why we consistently outperform in rebounding, year after year. Usually, after practice, they all ask me about the secret to our team's rebounding success over the years. The first thing I tell them is that there is no secret. If there were a secret, it would be that we instruct our players to aggressively go after the ball when it comes off the rim. If they knock someone down in their effort to do so, so be it. I try to explain that it's not about technique or strategy, but rather a mindset. I also share with them that they need to have the courage to conduct the war drill, or something similar, every day, without fear of injury, if they want their players to develop the toughness mentality required to become a consistently good rebounding team.

Usually, when I follow up with these coaches whom I had previously spoken to about our rebounding, they often say the same thing: "Coach G, we stopped playing *war* because we were afraid of getting our players injured." I then remind them of my advice about having the courage to overcome the fear of injury. Then, I inform them that in my 23 years at Michigan State, aside from some minor bumps and bruises, we've never had a player seriously injured while playing the *war* game.

The daily challenges that Tom puts our guys through eventually make them believe that they're tough because they've endured the rigors of Izzo's toughness training. Most importantly, once the transformation occurs, our players carry a mentality of toughness with them for the rest of their lives. For those of you who have always wondered, yes, we had our players engage in the "war game" during one of our practices while wearing helmets and shoulder pads.

During the 2001 season, I witnessed one of the most remarkable displays of toughness at any time during my entire coaching career. We were playing against Wisconsin at home, in a must-win game for the Big 10 title. The lead exchanged hands multiple times, and every possession was crucial to the final outcome of the game. About three or four days before the game, our star power forward Andre Hutson, also known as "Dre-Hut," wasn't feeling well. Our team doctors thoroughly examined him as soon as we learned about his condition, and they agreed that he should be ready to play on game day.

The game itself was an intense battle between two determined teams. Dre-Hut made significant plays for us on both offense and defense throughout the game. His performance that day was exactly what we expected from a star senior co-captain with the Big 10 Championship on the line.

During the final moments of the game, with only seconds left to play and our team holding onto a one-point lead, we desperately needed a stop on defense. Wisconsin had the ball for the final possession, with a chance to tie or make the game-winning shot. Unfortunately, we were unable to stop them. However, Dre-Hut came to our rescue with a spectacular defensive play that secured our victory.

In that crucial moment, he deflected a pass intended for the player he was guarding. He then chased down the loose ball and dove on the floor to gain possession just as time expired.

The exhilaration of the win led us to embrace each other in celebration. When I hugged Dre, I sensed something was off. His body felt weak, and it was evident that he was more fatigued than what would be expected from playing 38 minutes of a 40-minute game. Immediately after leaving the court, our team doctor, Jeff Kovan, advised Dre to shower and come to the training room for an examination. Dre's mother, Linda, our trainer T-Mac, equipment man Dave Pruder, Chief, and I all gathered in the training room to observe.

While Doc Kovan was examining Dre, it appeared that he was experiencing a seizure. Scared to our wits' end, we managed to get him off of the examining table and onto the floor without hurting him. As soon as we got him down, we began covering his entire body with ice to control the muscle spasms that were occurring throughout his entire body. Once the spasms were under control, Doc Kovan started an IV to replace the fluids he had lost during the game. It was later determined that the loss of fluids was the cause of the spasms, which initially appeared to be a seizure.

Additionally, after further examination, it was determined that, in addition to dehydration, he had pneumonia and had played the entire game at only 70% of his lung capacity.

I can't imagine the degree of mental and physical toughness it took for Dre to push through his illness and play at an elite level that night while being sick. It was an amazing feat of mind over matter. Looking back, I now realize that Dre didn't just want to win, he had to win. Since Dre's retirement from professional basketball, he has used that same must-win attitude to become a successful businessman in the greater Lansing Michigan area. If you want to have the must-win attitude of Andre Hutson, you must first cultivate a tough mentality, because without it, you won't be able to adhere to the daily discipline required to succeed (and win) in the game of life. I consider Andre to be naturally tough,

82

but as I mentioned earlier, it is also possible to develop a tough mentality.

To truly grasp the concept of toughness, it is important to understand the underlying characteristics that drive a person's mentality towards it. In general, the following characteristics define a person's mental toughness: courage, fear, desire, simplicity, and discipline. To fully appreciate how each of these characteristics can significantly impact one's mentality towards toughness, it is necessary to engage in honest self-evaluation. By honestly assessing oneself, a clear understanding of where one stands in relation to each of these five characteristics of toughness can be gained. However, self-evaluation can be challenging for many individuals. It is not easy for most people to look in the mirror and sincerely ask themselves, "Who am I?" and "Where do I stand in terms of personal growth?"

Let's begin by discussing courage and how it applies both in the game of basketball and in the game of life. You may have often heard that having courage doesn't mean you're never afraid; rather, it means that despite your fear, you are able to overcome it and take the necessary actions. In basketball, a clear example of conquering fear can be observed when an offensive player charges into a defensive player who positions his body directly in front of another oncoming player to prevent him from scoring an easy basket. This act requires great courage because the defensive player willingly sacrifices his own body by absorbing the impact of the collision, disregarding the fear of potential injury. This same scenario unfolds daily in the lives of individuals striving to succeed in the game of life.

We often fail to recognize small acts of courage because we become so absorbed in our own lives. These acts of courage happen every day, but we tend to overlook them or take them for granted. To illustrate this, let's consider the lives of coal miners in the past. These brave individuals would go underground every day, risking their lives to provide for their families. Back then, there were no safety regulations to protect them from the dangers of their work.

The point I'm making is that coal miners, like Andre Hutson, and individuals such as your next-door neighbor, share a similar level of immense toughness and courage. Regardless of the scale, both Andre Hutson and the coal miner had to display tremendous strength and bravery to overcome challenging circumstances.

In a similar vein, you can witness acts of courage and toughness in your own neighborhood. For example, your next-door neighbor, a father of six, works tirelessly for 16 hours a day to ensure a good life for his wife and children.

Each of these individual acts of toughness and courage serves as a reminder of the incredible demonstration of toughness and courage that I personally witnessed. It was when my son, Michael Ray, faced a life-threatening situation due to an infection that had developed while he was awaiting a heart transplant. In May 2021, after almost four years of waiting, his body became infected beneath his sternum, with the infection rapidly spreading towards his heart. If his doctors couldn't find a way to stop the infection or remove the metal LVAD device attached to his heart that kept it pumping, he would have lost his life.

Unfortunately, stopping the infection was not an option due to the presence of the metal LVAD device. Any foreign object, particularly metal, tends to attract infections within the body. Given the rapid progression of the infection, time was of the essence for his doctors to devise a solution. It's difficult for me to fully comprehend the exact plan that Dr. Weiss and his team of 101 physicians from around the world came up with, but it ultimately allowed my son to keep on living with only half a heart in his chest. In my mind, it was a GOD sent miracle.

On the morning of the surgery, Dr. Weiss visited our room to discuss the potential outcomes with Ray and me. Due to the unprecedented nature of the procedure, he explained that the odds of a successful surgery were against Ray. After providing a detailed explanation of the various possibilities, Dr. Weiss said to Ray, "Given the risks involved, I would understand if you decided not to proceed with the surgery. If that's what you're thinking, I can call it off, and hopefully, you'll be able to survive until you receive a heart transplant. However, I must inform you that time is limited for that to happen."

What impressed me the most about Ray was his response. Just as I was about to break down in tears, Ray sat up in bed, looked Dr. Weiss straight in the eye, and declared, "If you're ready, I'm ready. Let's go!" In that moment, Ray's unwavering determination and courage in the face of a life-threatening situation without any guarantees left me incredibly proud. Very few individuals could have managed a life-threatening situation like Ray did without experiencing an emotional breakdown.

In essence, regardless of the circumstances, the remedy for fear (False Evidence Appearing Real) is rooted in faith, toughness, and courage. When confronted with overwhelming odds and the potential loss of life or significant aspects of one's existence, such as love, family, career, or business, the mental image of losing everything can be incapacitating. To sustain the necessary resilience and bravery over an extended period, it is crucial to complement these qualities with unwavering determination to conquer insurmountable fear. In the face of life's hardships, trials, and tribulations, it is vital to maintain a simplified mindset. Avoid overanalyzing and complicating the situation. By keeping your thought processes clear and straightforward, you will cultivate the discipline needed to uphold the courage and resilience that will carry you through all the challenges you encounter on your unique life journey.

I firmly believe that timing and context are crucial in effectively utilizing toughness in life. Understanding when, where, and how to employ our toughness is essential. There are two types of toughness: aggressive and non-aggressive. Successful individuals in both life and basketball possess the ability to recognize when they need to be tough and determine the appropriate type of toughness required for each specific situation.

In basketball, aggressive toughness is exemplified when a player fearlessly dives to the floor to retrieve a loose ball, sets a solid screen, or competes for a rebound in a crowd of opponents without regard for their body. Aggressive toughness can also manifest verbally, such as when a team's leader uses a harsh tone to capture the attention of their teammates in critical moments during a game. In these instances, the leader may convey what the team needs to hear, rather than what they want to hear, in order to inspire them to perform at a high-performance maximum Xecution level.

The game of basketball provides numerous examples of both aggressive toughness and non-aggressive toughness. The examples are so abundant that it would require an entire book to cover them all. Let's explore a few instances.

One example of non-aggressive toughness is when a player takes a charge or skillfully avoids being hit by a screen, whether by going over it or under it, in order to maneuver around it. Another illustration is a player confidently making free throw shots under immense pressure with the game hanging in the balance. Additionally, when a player handles harsh criticism from a coach or teammate without reacting negatively, they demonstrate non-aggressive toughness.

During our journey to winning the National Championship in 2000, I personally witnessed two inspiring displays of both aggressive and non-aggressive toughness. In the Sweet Sixteen game against Syracuse, we found ourselves trailing by fourteen points at halftime. It was during this crucial moment that Mateen Cleaves exhibited aggressive toughness by passionately confronting and reprimanding his best friend and teammate, Morris Peterson.

Remarkably, Morris displayed a non-aggressive toughness by accepting the confrontation without retaliating. The significance of this interaction was magnified by the limited time available—only fifteen minutes—to address the issue. Mateen understood the urgency and acted promptly, demonstrating the importance of seizing the moment in such high-stakes situations. Mateen knew that if he couldn't quickly reach Pete and make him understand the need to step up his game in the second half, their chances of winning the National Championship would be lost. Many people fail to grasp that success or failure, whether in life or basketball, often hinges on critical decisions made within minutes or even seconds. Without a doubt, it was the shared toughness of Mateen and Pete during those crucial minutes in the locker room that secured us the National Championship and forever changed the history of Michigan State basketball. Moreover, the lives and legacies of every player and coach were positively transformed that day as a result of Mateen and Pete's shared toughness. The late great NBA superstar Bill Russell, a winner of 11 NBA world championships, once said, "The most important characteristic of a leader is toughness." I firmly believe that toughness is the core of one's character, ultimately leading to a successful life in any field—be it a superstar basketball player, a CEO, or parents raising their children to become successful and well-adjusted adults. Remember to always keep in mind the following five essential characteristics of toughness that drive your resilience.

The following are five key qualities to keep in mind: *courage, fear, desire, simplicity*, and *discipline*. These qualities reflect your level of toughness and determine how far you will go to achieve success in your life. Take some time to examine each characteristic and understand how it influences your toughness. This requires honest self-evaluation. It will also help you learn how, when, and where to effectively use *aggressive toughness* versus *non-aggressive toughness* to your advantage. Both types of toughness are equally important in your life's journey. You need both to navigate the inevitable tough times that arise from the hardships, trials, and tribulations we all face.

Remember the example of Mateen Cleaves and Morris Peterson in our locker room. Their situation could have become toxic and destroyed our chances of winning the game. However, they were able to appropriately use both *aggressive and non-aggressive toughness*, ultimately leading us to achieve our shared goal: winning the College Basketball National Championship. No matter what your specific national championship may be, believe me, it won't be easy. In fact, it's going to be challenging. The only way to overcome these challenges is to be *tough*!

Throughout the rest of your life keep in mind this OG'ism: *"if it ain't rough, it ain't right, and if it ain't tough, it ain't tight."*

Fundamental #7 – Playing with Intelligence

"Intelligence with toughness is lethal" Tom Izzo

Tom Izzo once shared with me the following insight: "A player who is tough is feared, but when they combine intelligence with toughness, they become a lethal weapon." Intelligent players, or individuals, understand that relying solely on talent and toughness is insufficient. Similarly, intelligence alone is not enough. To excel in the game of basketball or in life, it is crucial to grasp the importance of simplicity, game study, good judgment, minimizing mistakes, promptly rectifying errors, and maintaining a sense of urgency. Those who comprehend and effectively utilize these aspects of intelligence significantly enhance their chances of achieving success.

In my experience, the smartest players, whether in life or basketball, share a common belief: "Simplicity holds genius." For instance, Bill Gates amassed a fortune by simplifying computer usage, making it accessible to individuals of all ages, socio-economic backgrounds, and education levels. Similarly, top basketball players recognize the value of keeping the game simple. Legendary coach Pat Riley used a short, meaningful phrase to motivate his LA Laker teams before games, emphasizing the crucial factors for victory: "Play hard, play smart, play together."

The phrase exemplifies why Riley is regarded as a Hall of Fame coach and is currently considered the NBA's best general manager (GM). By closely examining his career, it becomes evident that Riley's intelligence played a key role in his success. He recognized that simply playing hard, being smart, or working together wasn't sufficient for consistent success. Instead, through years of trial and error, he discovered that combining all three elements unlocks the door to winning consistently. Coach Riley understood that by effectively conveying his integrative formula for success to the players, along with instilling the mindset that "enough is never enough," his teams would establish and maintain a winning culture.

In the game of basketball, the best players consistently exhibit high levels of intelligence. They understand that to excel and remain at the top, they need to possess extensive knowledge of every aspect of the game. This knowledge is acquired through countless hours of film study, allowing them to grasp advanced offensive and defensive concepts and strategies. Once they have a solid understanding of each facet, they must effectively apply that knowledge to consistently maximize their level of *High Performance Maximum Xecution.*

They understand that success will come if they do the right things. To illustrate this, let's consider a common scenario in today's game of basketball. Imagine a player trying to pass to his open teammate who is cutting to the rim for an easy score. However, instead of using a bounce pass, the player throws a chest pass, resulting in a turnover as a defensive player intercepts it. Although the player is aware of the proper technique for passing, his decision to use a chest pass instead of a bounce pass clearly shows that he is not yet capable of making intelligent decisions in such situations. The ability to make the right decision instantly, choosing the most appropriate pass, is the outcome of a player's dedication to studying game film and mastering fundamental skills.

Interestingly, we often witness similar scenarios unfold in life. Let's consider a hypothetical example: a person decides to establish a sports shoe brand like Nike, Adidas, or Jordan. He began by diligently researching the manufacturing process and costs associated with producing the shoes, as well as the potential profits from each sale. He felt confident that he had invested the necessary time and effort to become an expert in manufacturing athletic shoes.

However, he overlooked the importance of dedicating equal time to researching sales and marketing strategies, which are crucial for business growth and profitability. Despite his lack of knowledge in sales and marketing, he proceeded to manufacture and sell his shoes, resulting in unexpected challenges. The failure of his business was not due to a lack of demand for his quality shoes, but rather a lack of comprehensive preparation. By taking shortcuts and neglecting to develop a well-thought-out marketing strategy, he ultimately led his business to failure. If he had taken the time to intelligently plan and implement effective marketing tactics, he might have been able to sustain his company. Unfortunately, his inadequate preparation in the marketing aspect quickly led to insufficient sales, ultimately causing the downfall of his business. The downfall of the company wasn't due to a poorly manufactured shoe that customers refused to buy. Instead, the failure originated from inadequate marketing efforts.

As Pat Riley wisely stated, the company didn't approach the "game" - in this case, the business - with sufficient intelligence or strategy. The company disrespected the necessary process to achieve success in the athletic shoe industry, mistakenly thinking that expertise in shoe manufacturing alone would ensure success in shoe sales. If there had been a more profound understanding of the entire marketing process before attempting to sell the shoes, the outcome might have been different. Acquiring marketing expertise would have enabled the company to capitalize on its capacity to produce quality shoes. People often mistakenly assume that if they can master one aspect of their profession, they will achieve success. However, mastering a single facet requires understanding and mastering its smaller components.

This is what I term as a 'position-based' approach. Let's consider basketball as an example. If I'm a power forward, I can build a successful career by focusing solely on becoming an expert rebounder. In this position, I'm not expected to understand the complexities of other roles or lead the team. However, if I'm a point guard, which is like a company's CEO, I need to grasp the intricacies of all positions because my role involves leading the team. In the basketball world, the point guard is often referred to as the coach on the floor, given that the coach can't be on the floor during the game.

Similarly, the shoe salesman made a similar error. If the basketball player had considered broadening his understanding of the game, he would have known how to execute the right pass at the right time during the game. Furthermore, he could have maximized the use of his unique talent or "superpower."

Winners in life or on the basketball court always avoid the pitfall of thoughtless action. Success requires intelligent planning and execution in any endeavor. Once you have meticulously planned your course of action, seek advice from those who have traveled the path before you. Don't let ego hinder you from gaining wisdom from others' experiences. Remember, knowledge, intelligence, and experience are irreplaceable assets for anyone aiming for success. If you're looking to boost your IQ, specifically in regards to your understanding of basketball or life, it's essential to realize that neither life nor basketball can be effectively navigated without thoughtful consideration. Avoiding a mindless approach requires a significant investment of time into cultivating the intellectual expertise needed to thoroughly master your chosen pursuit. Once you've gained the necessary knowledge and skills, it's crucial to use them wisely to construct a comprehensive strategy or business plan. This will allow you to perform at an exceptional level in your chosen field. However, even the most well-crafted plan won't succeed unless you can apply good judgment when executing it, especially during challenging times.

Remember that poor judgment often stems from insufficient knowledge and experience, which can lead to costly mistakes that could disrupt or even ruin your success. While mistakes are part of the learning process, intelligent individuals in both basketball and life strive to prevent errors wherever possible and are ready to swiftly alleviate the effects of unexpected ones.

The number of individuals who reach the top of their respective fields is extremely small. This is because the margin of error for achieving ultimate success is so slim that many people struggle to comprehend it. Those who are intelligent enough understand that to conquer this tiny margin of error, they must be willing to endure the struggles that come with the pursuit of success. They know that when the margin for error is small, the need for urgency is high.

This principle becomes evident when you study the traits of highly successful individuals. Take "Chief," for example, a coach whose sense of urgency and meticulous attention to detail outshines those of any other coach in the country. His life is filled with a constant sense of urgency that might seem to others like he's always in high gear. This intense approach, if not properly managed, can lead to perpetual stress—a level that many people are unprepared to handle.

However, Chief's sense of urgency is different from that of most people. He doesn't view his intense approach to life as a source of stress. Instead, he sees his high-energy lifestyle as an ally that aids him in his daily quest to consistently achieve success at the highest level.

However, this high sense of urgency comes at a cost: a fast-paced lifestyle that not everyone can handle. These individuals also dedicate countless hours to evaluating themselves and developing in-depth strategies to stay at the top of their professions. The characteristics of highly successful people are numerous and continuous, which is why the same individuals, companies, and teams tend to consistently stay on top. In simpler terms, life is challenging.

Statistics reveal that 95% of people never experience a significant level of success throughout their entire lives, leading to the startling fact that only 5% of the world's population owns 95% of its wealth. This is because the remaining 95% of us are unwilling to maintain the necessary level of urgency and dedication required to reach and sustain high-level success. For those of you who truly aspire to belong to the 5% who possess the majority of the world's wealth, it is crucial to understand the importance of maintaining a high sense of urgency.

High achievers often possess a unique characteristic: they approach things from a different perspective compared to most people. They think outside the box and constantly seek innovative ways to increase their chances of success. Their unwavering drive to win is a healthy one because it fuels their passion for life.

One of the key factors contributing to Tom Izzo's success is his ability to recognize the potential in others and help them achieve greatness. He has honed this trait through self-evaluation and has dedicated his life's work to empowering people to pursue their dreams, just as he has lived his own. This philosophy is shared by other highly successful individuals like Earvin "Magic" Johnson and Draymond "DayDay" Green, who have realized that prioritizing the success of others in both basketball and life ultimately leads to their own success. However, their journey wouldn't have been possible without their willingness to learn, embrace simplicity, exercise good judgment, and seek guidance. These qualities have enabled them to effectively leverage their remarkable talents and increase their likelihood of success.

Although all three men possess high intelligence, they are not inherently more intelligent than the average person. The key distinction between them and most individuals lies in their deliberate choice to utilize their intelligence in pursuit of their goals, dreams and aspirations.

Another common characteristic among intelligent individuals is their willingness to listen to others and genuinely consider their input. Contrary to popular belief, Tom Izzo is not a dictator; he actively listens to his players and coaches. However, he reserves his attention for those individuals whom he trusts or shares a genuine relationship with. This may contribute to the misperception of him being an authoritarian figure, as spectators often witness him passionately engaging with his players during games. In reality, what may appear as uncontrolled anger is actually Tom strategically channeling his emotions.

What the public often fails to witness is the extensive amount of time and effort Tom invests in building relationships with his players long before any confrontational moments occur. He dedicates considerable hours to understanding their motivations, level of self-motivation, and their capacity to be pushed to achieve success and reach their goals. He starts by explaining in detail to his players what it will take to achieve their goals and how he can assist them in reaching those goals. Then, he asks for their permission to push them to become high-performance maximum Xecution players.

Only if they agree to his offer, will you see him become more assertive with that player. This specific aspect of his coaching philosophy, which I refer to as "Relationships Driven Leadership," is the undeniable foundation behind his 23 years of continuous coaching success.

While Chief possesses one of the greatest basketball minds in the history of the game, he never boasts about his skills as an X & O coach. Instead, he takes pride in dedicating more time to his players than any other coach in the business. Once again, the secret to his success lies in the simple concept of investing time, which is a crucial element of Relationship Driven Leadership.

I have no doubt in my mind that Tom's belief in Relationship-Driven Leadership was the decisive factor that led us to win the national championship in 2000. He demonstrated this belief in action during our Elite 8 game against Iowa State, which proved to be the toughest game throughout our championship journey. I believed they were the second-best team in the country that year.

In that game, we found ourselves trailing by 8 points with a little under two minutes left to play. However, we made an incredible comeback towards the end of the game, putting ourselves in a position to win. To accomplish that, we needed a crucial basket to either tie or take the lead. That's when Tom called a timeout to set up a play.

Initially, he designed the play for Morris Peterson to take the shot, but after reviewing the play, he quickly noticed the negative body language of our players. Immediately, he encouraged them to voice their frustrations with the play intended for Pete. The conversation in the huddle unfolded as follows:

"What the f***'s wrong?" At that moment, Mateen Cleaves placed his hand over the whiteboard and erased the play Tom had drawn up for Pete. He suggested, "Let's get the ball into Dre (Andre Hutson)," who was usually our fifth offensive option. Mateen's reasoning for choosing Dre was based on the fact that he had scored the last three baskets that had brought us back and put us in a position to win the game.

However, the players' desire to get Dre the ball made Tom uncomfortable, just as his decision made them feel uneasy about Pete taking the shot. After Tom ultimately decided to get the ball to Dre, he challenged him to make the shot. He explicitly stated, "Okay, I'll get you the ball, but you better make the shot." Dre, a man of few words, looked Tom directly in the eye and responded, "Get me the ball." That's when Tom devised the play for him. However, before he could finalize it, Mateen once again placed his hand on the whiteboard and erased the play. The original plan involved Mo Pete passing the ball to Dre, but Pete wasn't known for his exceptional passing skills. On the other hand, passing was Mateen's greatest strength. Anticipating Tom's frustration, Mateen explained, "I'll make the pass," while erasing the portion of the play involving Pete's pass. As our team left the huddle, their body language clearly exhibited their trust in Dre's ability to make the shot.

They proceeded onto the court and flawlessly executed the play exactly as Tom had designed it. Dre confidently made the crucial shot, just as his teammates had trusted him to do, and the rest is now part of history. In a high-stakes game, when we needed high-performance maximum execution, it was Chief's relationship-based leadership that guided the trust he placed in the thoughts and abilities of his players.

Personally, I have always admired Tom's playing system because it challenges the racist stereotype that black basketball players are only exceptional physical specimens with athleticism but lack the intelligence required to excel in a sophisticated basketball system. This racist mindset has often been used against us during recruiting, where competing schools would tell prospective players, "Don't choose Michigan State because they run too many plays, and you won't be able to showcase your skills." It is unquestionably a backhanded racist statement. If the players and parents of these recruits, particularly those who are African American, took the time to reflect on what this statement truly implies, they would realize that it is a veiled insult to the intelligence of their young men.

What is actually being portrayed is that their young men lack the necessary intelligence to thrive in a system that demands strategic thinking. However, these same coaches claim that they prepare players to succeed in the NBA. I find this amusing because NBA coaches often emphasize a player's basketball IQ or the absence thereof. The tragedy lies in the fact that many talented players are denied the opportunity to play in the NBA because they were never taught how to utilize their intelligence to play the game effectively. Furthermore, it angers me even more to think about how many of these coaches, who perpetuate this mindset, fail to recognize their own racist thinking. As Dr. Martin Luther King once said, the two most dangerous things in the world are "sincere ignorance and conscientious stupidity."

CHAPTER TWO

Characteristic #2 – Talent

"Talent Is Never Enough"

Branden BJ Dawson

Of all the distinguishing qualities associated with successful basketball teams, Fortune 500 companies, and a wide variety of sports teams and business organizations, the most sought-after trait by all of them is undeniably *talent*. Why? Because talent can be a significant factor in determining success. However, it's important to remember that *talent alone is never enough* to ensure a high level of sustainable success. When talent is properly developed, it can be an enormous advantage. However, when talent is not properly developed, it becomes a disadvantage. I've seen this scenario play out many times, where motivated, hard-working individuals who may not be the most talented outperform unmotivated, extremely talented individuals. This happens whenever there is an absence of the following *seven intangible winning traits:* Hard Work (hard worker), Self-Motivation, Intensity, Energy, Enthusiasm, Passion, and Competitive Drive. When ordinary people use their measure of God-given talent and combine it with these *seven intangible winning traits*, they often live a life filled with extraordinary success.

That's why just having a high measure of talent alone is rarely enough to achieve a sustainable level of high-performance maximum Xecution play. Unfortunately, God doesn't equally gift each one of us with the same measure of talent. However, what he does equally gift us all with is the intellectual capacity to utilize the 7 intangible winning traits that enhance our chances of success despite our measure of talent. The utilization of the 7 intangible winning traits isn't complex or hard to understand; rather, it's merely nothing more than making the simple choice to live a lifestyle that exercises the use of these traits daily. The decision to live your life in correlation with the 7 intangible winning traits is the first step towards turning your measure of talent, no matter how big or small, into your superpower. God has created us all as free-willed human beings with the liberty to make our own decisions. Therefore, the decision to make your life whatever you want it to be is ultimately in your own hands. Believe me, if you're willing to adopt the 7 intangible winning traits as a way of life. You'll see your measure of *talent*, *manifest* itself into a *superpower* that will forever turn your life into a multitude of abundance and blessings.

We're all gifted with a special talent of some sort; however, "talent" is relative and cannot be measured on the same scale for every person. I would have considered myself a very talented basketball player in my day. In fact, my talent earned me a scholarship to play college basketball at Northern Michigan University. On the other hand, my measure of talent wouldn't come close to matching that of an extremely talented player like Michael Jordan or LeBron James. The problem with this fluid definition of talent is the disconnect it creates when people measure their talent against an uneven standard. Consequently, many people compare themselves to extremely gifted individuals, which results in them downplaying their own talent. The realization of this can be disheartening and can often be the reason people give up on their hopes and dreams. Yet, the opposite logic can be true because, in reality, a lot of people especially those who rely solely on their talent, often overestimate their actual level of talent. This phenomenon, known as "talent shock," is frequently observed among incoming freshmen who play their first year of big-time college basketball. In high school, these players were likely the most talented individuals on their team, in their city, and even in their state. However, once they arrive on campus, they find themselves surrounded by a group of players who were the most talented in their respective town, city or state. When this reality sets in, the players who go on to become great are the ones who quickly realize that talent alone is not enough. They develop an immediate appreciation for the value of hard work and the importance of other intangible winning traits.

Harnessing your talent is just as important as actually possessing the talent. Part of that process is to become creative with how you utilize your talent. In my case, I decided to combine my basketball talent and my passion for teaching, becoming a basketball coach. Surprisingly, it's a profession I never really had any interest in. Similarly, a talented singer may choose to focus their passion for music into songwriting or music production, especially if their vocal talent doesn't measure up to the best of the best. There are also situations where a person's talent in one area can develop into untapped talent in another area. A great example of this is former NBA players Dave Bing, former Mayor of Detroit, and Kevin Johnson, former Mayor of Sacramento. They both utilized the leadership and discipline they developed while playing professional basketball to effectively govern their cities. In both cases, these gentlemen were extraordinarily talented basketball players who realized that their greatest talents beyond the game of basketball were leadership and drive. Success stories like Bing's and Johnson's further demonstrate the importance of harnessing your talent in a focused and creative way.

As I previously mentioned, God gives everyone some form of talent; however, the measure of talent is not equally dispersed. There are people who are blessed with extraordinary talent that greatly exceeds the measure of talent God has given others. These people have unique physical or mental attributes that enhance their ability to perform at an almost superhuman level, which is unattainable for most people. However, even these gifted few stand to benefit from doing a few things that will help them capitalize on their amazing abilities.

If you recall, I also previously mentioned that no matter your measure of talent, it is important to embrace the 7 intangible winning traits. These traits have been proven to be the difference in transforming an extremely talented individual into an extremely successful one. I've decided to add an additional word to a couple of my original 7 intangible winning traits. I did this to better emphasize the magnitude of their power in influencing success. Now they are as follows:1) Hard Worker 2) Self-Motivation and Discipline 3) Passion 4) Intensity, Energy & Enthusiasm 5) Confidence & Competitive Drive 6) Leadership 7) G.U.T.S. (Glory Under Tough Situations)

Draymond Green, or "DayDay" as he is called by his closest friends, is a great example of someone who exemplifies the theory that talent alone is never enough. In 2012, Draymond was drafted 34th by the Golden State Warriors, and today he can name every player that was taken in front of him. However, based on his body of work to date, he would probably be the first or second player taken if that same draft were held today. Looking back at his first few seasons in the league, it's very clear that statistically his numbers at that time were comparable, and in some instances superior, to the top players at his position in the NBA. Although those numbers were off the charts statistically, it wasn't the numbers that made him a special player. Instead, it's his intangible winning traits that make him one of the most unique players to ever play in the NBA. The value of intangible winning traits cannot be measured solely by numbers (statistics), but they are important factors in terms of what Draymond brings to his team's winning equation. Most NBA experts would agree that his raw talent is very insignificant in comparison to his leadership and other six intangible winning traits.

His unique ability to make other players around him better is a gift that very few players have. As a senior co-captain at Michigan State, I watched him convince a team made up of slightly above average players that if they genuinely embraced the seven *intangible winning traits*, they could win a championship. That team went on to win both the 2012 regular season Big10 conference and tournament championships. Draymond's vision for that team wasn't based on some hypothetical or illusional hype speech. Instead, he based his belief on what he had experienced playing on other championship teams at Michigan State in the past.

Those teams had achieved what he had envisioned for this team by collectively embracing the seven *intangible winning traits* that ultimately led to success, regardless of a team's measure of talent. The same *intangible winning traits* that have been instrumental in shaping Draymond Green's successful basketball career are the same intangible traits that define his leadership style and contribute to his team's success.

Winning traits that lend themselves to success in the game of life. Early on in the chapter, I talked about the importance of both harnessing and being able to creatively combine one of your talents with another one of your talents. Draymond has done just that, taking his basketball talents and combining them with his incredible leadership qualities and other intangible winning traits to make them the cornerstones of a successful career. His creative combination of talents has allowed him to achieve things in basketball that he never dreamed possible.

His critics said that he was too fat and too slow to play at Michigan State. Obviously, his accomplishments have proven them all wrong because his college career at Michigan State speaks for itself. During his time at Michigan State, he was a three-year starter, two-time team captain, an All-Big Ten 1st team player, Big Ten MVP, and first-team All-American. Today, his hard work and determination have enabled him to be recognized as one of the NBA's most highly regarded players, a status that has earned him a very lucrative contract with the Golden State Warriors, where he has been a starting player for the Warriors' four-time

NBA World Championship team. He is also a three-time NBA All-Star and an Olympic Gold Medal Winner. In fact, these accolades positioned him to be one of the most sought-after players on the NBA free agent market following his 2015 season. His earning potential at that time increased rapidly from sixty-four million to eighty-five million dollars. However, the Golden State Warriors regarded his intangible winning traits as so valuable to their team's continued success that they decided to renegotiate his current eighty-five million dollar five-year contract and re-sign him to a new four-year, one-hundred-million-dollar deal.

The moment Draymond hypothetically signed his hundred-million-dollar contract, he literally surpassed many players with a higher measure of talent, which speaks to the fact that talent alone is never enough. The failure of those players was not due to a lack of talent, but rather their unwillingness to genuinely embrace the seven intangible winning traits needed to transform their talent into a superpower that would manifest itself into a level of high-performance, maximum Xecution. That would have allowed them to fully take advantage of their talent. In blunt terms, the acquisition of these intangible winning traits is your choice. It requires a conscious decision to make them a part of your daily lifestyle.

Tom Izzo likes to talk about success in terms of what he calls the three L's. He believes that most people like the success they pursue, some love it, but there are only a special few who are willing to live what they must do to be successful. To effectively summon your superpower, you have to live in total coexistence with the intangible winning traits every day. Inherently, most people know the value of these traits and how important they are in regards to success, yet they're either unwilling or too lazy and undisciplined to execute them daily.

Consequently, a lot of talented people don't succeed because they don't want to embrace the pressure and responsibility associated with a life of success. They know that if they accept that responsibility, they would be expected to perform at their highest level all the time. Many of them are capable of handling that responsibility based solely on their talent alone but aren't committed to going the extra mile to achieve the highest level of success. "Going the extra mile" is a quote often used in the world of sports that indicates putting in extra time, effort, and meaningful work.

The equivalent of going the extra mile in the game of life would be something as simple as being the first person in the office every morning and the last one to leave every day. Another example would be packing four years of college credits into two and a half years in order to eliminate debt. Comparatively, unlike Draymond, there are some very talented players in the game of basketball who are "60%'ers". Inconceivably, these players' 60% effort is better than the average player's (person's) 100% effort. The first time I ever heard effort described this way was when I was talking with Erik Kapitulek, the Founder and CEO of a team-building organization called The Program. His staff consisted of retired Navy Seals and Special Forces veterans. In 2014, we had the opportunity to have them work with our team. One day, after they had put our team through one of their grueling sessions, I asked Erik what he thought of our most talented player, (BJ) Branden Dawson. His answer was something I had never heard before in my life. His thoughts forever changed the way I evaluate talent. What he said to me was something that I had never thought of before in terms of a person's measure of talent.

He said that BJ was a victim of his own TALENT, because throughout his playing career, he'd been able to accomplish things on the basketball court without giving maximum effort. He said what was most damaging to his college career was the fact that BJ was able to become a McDonalds All-American, a honor given to the top twenty best high school basketball players in the country, with just giving only 60% effort. Erik believed that the repercussions of this would set him up to ultimately fail if he didn't change his mindset. He further explained that this happen to BJ because the level of effort he gave throughout high school had falsely ingrained in his mind that his 60% effort was all out effort and good enough to play at a *High Performance Maximum Xecution Level* as a college and professional player. Thank goodness BJ had the opportunity to be teammates with some guys that had tremendous work ethic ,Draymond Green(Golden State Warriors) for a year and Gary Harris (Denver Nuggets) and Denzel Valentine (Chicago Bulls) for two years. All these guys are currently NBA players largely because of their work ethic, willingness to accept the responsibility and pressure associated with giving the game 100% every day.

Fortunately for BJ, the light bulb finally went on during the summer of his senior year in 2015. During that season, he played well enough to have thirteen double-doubles (double-figure points and double-figure rebounds) out of our eighteen Big 10 Conference games. This was an incredible feat at any level of basketball, whether it be high school, college, or the pros. In fact, his improved level of play was a major factor in getting us to the 2015 Final Four.

However, his outstanding play that season wasn't enough to overcome his previous three years of average play at best, considering his measure of talent. Although he was an extremely gifted player capable of being a great NBA player, NBA teams wanted to see more from him. Unfortunately, most NBA teams lacked the confidence that he would play up to his high level of potential. As a result, no team took a chance on drafting him until the very bottom of the draft.

Disappointingly, out of the 60 players taken in the 2015 draft, he was picked 56th overall by the LA Clippers. As it is often said, God sometimes works in mysterious ways because Branden's low draft status turned out to be both a blessing and a curse. It was a curse because his draft status was much lower than he or anyone else expected, but it was a blessing because it forced him into a situation where he had to finally commit to the seven intangible winning traits that are necessary to play at a high-performance maximum Xecution level every day, as previously stated. That summer, his willingness to shift his attitude upgraded his performance enough that he was able to average a double-double in the July NBA summer pro league in Orlando, Florida. His performance during the summer league reframed the team's thoughts about him, and as a result, he put himself in a position to sign a two-year deal with the L.A. Clippers for $500,000.00 a year guaranteed. This kind of deal is typically never offered to a player picked 56th in the draft. All of this came about because he finally realized that his talent alone wasn't enough.

INTANGIBLE WINNING TRAIT ONE

TALENT HAS TO WORK HARD (BE A HARD WORKER)

Denzel Valentine

It was the fall of 2015, around 8:00 AM, when we walked into our office as a staff to begin the workday. The first thing we typically heard was the sound of the beep as we pushed the fingerprint scanner to let ourselves into the building. We could still smell the fresh scent in the air as we entered our newly renovated offices. Next, we would hear the sound of a ball bouncing and catch a whiff of sweat from the gym below. These were the sounds and smells we encountered every day as we entered our basketball offices each morning. The astounding thing about these early morning encounters was that the ball had already been bouncing for at least two hours before we arrived. The sound of the ball bouncing was evidence of another one of Denzel Valentine's early morning workouts.

It had always been Denzel's dream to be a Spartan basketball player like his dad, Carlton, who played under Jud Heathcote from 1985 to 1988. During my twenty-three years at Michigan State, I had the opportunity to see the work ethic of many great players, and I can say without a doubt that Denzel's work ethic matches them all and, in some cases, even exceeds many of them.

As a matter of fact, he was so determined to have a special season his senior year that he elevated his already great work ethic to an elite level. Zel's story is incredible because he went from being considered undraftable to becoming a lottery pick in the 2016 NBA Draft for the Chicago Bulls. Coach Izzo once quoted, "Denzel is probably the hardest working player I've ever coached." His early morning individual workouts, extra lifts, and conditioning speak volumes about what it truly means to be a hard worker, as opposed to someone who simply works hard. Many people work hard, but there are very few who are truly hard workers. The difference between a hard worker and someone who merely works hard is that hard workers are never satisfied with the quantity, quality, or precision of their work. On the other hand, people who just work hard aren't lazy; they give maximum effort to the task at hand but are satisfied with the time, effort, and quality of their work.

They have NO interest in doing anything more than what they're told. *Hard Workers* like Denzel understand the value of being a *Hard Worker*. He understood that if his competitors were running two extra miles after practice, then he needed to run three extra miles after practice. If his opponents were making 500 shots a day, then he needed to make 1000 shots a day. Denzel's *Hard Worker* mentality is a common denominator found among all successful people, whether that success is in the game of life or basketball. The blueprint is always the same. The principal elements of this blueprint are made up of the *seven intangible winning traits* that I've discussed in the previous chapter. As I have mentioned before, they are as follows: *Hard Worker*, Self-Motivation and Discipline, Passion, Intensity-Energy and

Enthusiasm, Leadership, Confidence, Competitive Drive, and G.U.T.S. Of all the *seven intangible winning traits*, how ironic is it that Denzel is most notably recognized as a *Hard Worker*. More than any other trait, it is his relentless allegiance to being a *Hard Worker* that made him an NBA player, in spite of his limited measure of talent. Denzel, like most *Hard Workers*, knows that he may not be the most talented person in his particular field. However, he also knows that talent can be the most overrated characteristic needed to be successful. Yet, talent is still the most sought-after human resource on the planet, but it can be outworked by its competition if the talent isn't properly developed and has no interest in adhering to my seven intangible winning traits. This mismanagement of talent happens because most people think that life provides an overwhelming advantage to the guy who has the most talent. In reality, only when there is a commitment to being a *Hard Worker* can talent be an advantage.

In an effort to stay ahead of their competitors, *Hard Workers* continuously evaluate the work ethic of their competitors because they know that they can't stay ahead if they are being outworked. *Hard Workers* believe that in order to be the best, they must have the best work ethic. They understand that there is no substitute for putting in extra time and effort to perfect their craft. A classic example of this is Denzel's decision, after his freshman season, to spend hours practicing shooting because he wasn't a good consistent shooter. Looking back, by the time he was a senior, he not only became a good shooter but also an impressive clutch shooter, all because he dedicated extra time to working on his shooting skills. In the context of life, putting in extra work may involve attending networking events, practicing interview skills with a friend, acquiring additional job training, taking extra courses to enhance education, or meeting with a career counselor/coach after work.

Hard Workers understand that their talent alone will only give them a slight edge over their competition, making them a few seconds faster or able to jump a couple of inches higher. Let's use the game of football as an example to better illustrate how closely talent is measured among competitors in terms of *High Performance Maximum Xecution* level play, and what it is not in the world of athletics.

In football, for instance, there is a significant difference in the speed of players who run the 40-yard dash in 4.7 seconds and those who run it in 4.5 seconds, despite there being only two tenths of a second between their times. What may appear as a small difference in speed actually translates to a tremendous disparity in game performance. The capabilities of a player with 4.5 speed on the field, compared to a player with 4.7 speed, are light years apart. The mere two tenths of a second enable the faster player to run 50 yards from the goal line and score a touchdown without being caught, whereas the slower player may only manage to run for 10 yards before being tackled by the opposing team.

However, a slower player who is a *Hard Worker* can outperform the faster player if he is not willing to put in the extra time to properly develop his superior talent. The slower player has to focus on developing the finer aspects of the game at a high-performance, maximum Xecution level to compensate for his lack of speed if he wants to compete with the faster player.

What I mean by "small things" is understanding field position, down and distance, and route execution, if he is a receiver. However, truthfully speaking, that doesn't matter if the other player (person) with the superior measure of *talent* takes on the *hard workers mentality*. If the player with the superior measure of *talent* does take on a *hard worker's mentality*, it is almost impossible for the player of *less talent* to level the playing field through sheer *hard work*. Still, in light of *talent* giving one player an enormous advantage over another player, *hard work* is still a significant factor in determining *High Performance Maximum*

Xecution Play, no matter a player's (person's) measure of *talent*, large or small. Players that are *Elite High Performance Maximum Xecution* performers understand that it is the *combination* of *hard work* and *God-given talent* that makes their gift special and that one without the other isn't enough to benefit from their *talent*.

If you research the lives of basketball's greatest players like Kobe Bryant, Magic Johnson, Larry Bird, Kevin Durant, Derrick Rose, Kevin Love, LeBron James, Steph Curry, or Russell Westbrook, what you will most likely discover is that the common denominator among each one of them is high-level talent and an elite-level work ethic. The lesson to learn here is that high-level talent is not necessary to cultivate an elite-level work ethic. Contrary to our unequal measure of talent, our measure of work ethic, on the other hand, is our choice because God has made us all free-will human beings with the privilege of determining our own choices. I believe elite work ethic, in combination with the 7 intangible winning traits, gives hard workers a solid platform from which they can successfully achieve 95% of their life's ambitions. The best example of a hard worker's climb to success is Tom Izzo. He's that ordinary everyday hard-working guy who carved out a Hall of Fame coaching career and built a perennial nationally ranked basketball program by demanding high-performance maximum Xecution of his players.

He came from a place, as he likes to say, where there are "nine months of winter and one month of bad sledding," called Iron Mountain, a small mining town in the Upper Peninsula of Michigan. It isn't an easy place to come from and make it big. But when you grow up in a tough environment, it will either break you or teach you how to be tough, fight for what you want, and, most of all, how to be a hard worker. It wasn't an easy road for Chief when he came down here from the Upper Peninsula to work for Jud Heathcote as a graduate assistant. Right from the beginning, Jud was ruthlessly hard on Tom. He made sure Tom understood how he felt about him, and every day he said and did things to express his opinion. Jud told him countless times that he should quit because he wasn't cut out to be a coach anywhere, especially at the college level. It's one thing to say that to someone if you're trying to motivate them, but if you knew Jud, he said it because he meant every word without remorse, and trust me, it was meant to be hurtful. Despite Jud's efforts to break him, Chief overcame it all and became the coach that Jud said he couldn't become.

But more importantly, the man he is today is because the small-town guy did have what it takes to make it big time. Chief is the perfect example of why you can't judge a book by its cover. Looking back, there were always three things about him that were undeniable: his passion, his self-motivation, discipline and above all else, he was and still is a hard worker. Those are three of my seven intangible winning traits that, in combination, regardless of a person's measure of talent, serve as a blueprint for success.

INTANGIBLE WINNING TRAIT TWO
TALENT HAS TO BE SELF MOTIVATED AND DISCIPLINE
Bryn Forbes

To be a high-performance maximum Xecution achiever, even the most talented players (people) must be profoundly self-motivated and disciplined. Most players (people) unwittingly don't realize that there is a significant difference between motivation and self-motivation. Motivation is driven by external influences, such as another person influencing you to push yourself to work at a level higher than you would be willing to without their external motivation. These external influencers are usually people you trust or at least have respect for, like a boss, parent, preacher, teacher, or coach. In most cases, this person's influence on you is usually because they're in a position of authority. Conversely, self-motivation is internally driven, and players (people) that are internally motivated usually become high-performance maximum

Xecution achievers. Players (people) that are internally motivated don't need the influence of someone else's motivation to be hard workers. People that are self-motivated are willing to do the extra, no matter what that extra might be in terms of their particular ambitions. They're willing to go to work early and stay late, take on additional assignments, and strive to work, no matter the task, at a high-performance maximum Xecution level every day.

Throughout my college coaching career, the players who have been most successful are those who have been self-motivated and disciplined. Among these players, the majority who exhibit self-motivation and discipline usually go on to become professional players, unless they are hindered by injury or unforeseen circumstances. Individuals such as Shawn Respert, Eric Snow, Maurice Ager, Alan Anderson, Paul Davis, Kevin Willis, Shannon Brown, Greg Kelser, Draymond Green, Adreian Payne, Steve Smith, Zach Randolph, Jaron Jackson, Miles Bridges, Gary Harris, Denzel Valentine, Gabe Brown, Mateen Cleaves, Bryn Forbes, and Magic Johnson are all examples of players who have displayed self-motivation and discipline throughout their careers. While each player's professional path has been somewhat different, the common denominator among them all is self-motivation. Among the players I previously mentioned, Bryn Forbes stands out as the individual who best embodies the description of a highly driven, self-motivated, and disciplined player that I have had the privilege of coaching. Furthermore, he is by far the best shooter I have ever coached.

Bryn came to Michigan State as a transfer from Cleveland State. We decided to take him largely based on the recommendation of his best friend and teammate, Denzel Valentine. They were both teammates at Lansing Sexton High School and were part of a team that won back-to-back State Championships. Their high school coach, Carlton Valentine, who also played at Michigan State in the '80s, is Zel's dad. Unlike many college basketball players who transfer, Bryn didn't have to sit out a year at Michigan

State before playing. The NCAA granted him an exception to the transfer rule because his sister was critically ill and he had a newborn baby boy who needed his attention in Lansing, Michigan. Once he committed to returning home to play for us at Michigan State, he had to face the reality of dealing with tough personal responsibilities and circumstances on a daily basis. Another reality he had to face after committing to us was giving up significant playing time and his starting position at Cleveland State. When you think about it, the fact that he chose to commit to us without any guarantee of playing time, considering we already had a deep team filled with talented players, speaks volumes about his confidence and character.

Although he was an outstanding player at CSU, he was nowhere near ready to play any significant minutes on a top-25, nationally ranked Big Ten team. When he first arrived, his body just wasn't ready to meet the demands that would be placed on it throughout a rigorous Big Ten season. However, fortunately for him, his strength was shooting the ball, which happened to be our team's weakness at the time. But at Michigan State, you have to earn your playing time; no one sees the floor simply based on a single talent alone. Bryn needed to become more than just an elite shooter. He would have to adapt and become proficient at the staples rooted in the Michigan State Basketball culture: defending, rebounding, and running. However, to his detriment, defending was the one aspect he knowingly struggled with initially.

Even though Bryn had a mountain of obstacles to overcome, he remained disciplined and committed to becoming the best basketball player his God-given talent would allow. Bryn knew from the beginning that it would be difficult to earn playing time or a spot in our playing group. Which meant he would have to put in a lot of extra work in addition to our daily two-hour practices, 30-minute strength and conditioning sessions, four-day-a-week film sessions, academic study sessions, and, of course, attending classes. Even at that, if he wasn't a self-motivated, disciplined hard worker, the task would have been literally impossible because the work commitment would have been too monumental for him to overcome. The resolve it takes to sustain this level of commitment on a daily basis for an extended period of time requires you to be not only self-motivated but also self-disciplined. The reason being is that you won't be motivated every day to do the extra work hard if you don't have the self-discipline to push yourself on those days when you don't have the motivation to do the work. That's why someone else can't want it for you more than you want it for yourself. As a matter of fact, as I previously mentioned, if you're not self-motivated, the pressure will beat you down both mentally and physically until you submit to quitting. But because Bryn didn't quit and was incredibly self-motivated and self-disciplined, he was able to beat the odds and eventually became a starting player for us, playing 26 minutes a game, while shooting 44.7% overall, 42.7% from the three-point field goal range, 80% from the free-throw line, and averaging 8.5 points a game on our 2015 Final Four team.

The stories of self-motivated people aren't exclusive to professional basketball players like Bryn Forbes. One such story is that of Gregory Eaton, a Lansing, Michigan businessman. Gregory's story is a rags-to-riches tale that begins with him starting a cleaning company while working out of the back of his old, second-hand station wagon. He and his wife built their cleaning company while holding full-time jobs at the local Oldsmobile factory. Through their hard work and sacrifices, they were able to transform their mom-and-pop startup cleaning business into a well-established, profitable company.

Gregory, like all savvy businessmen, wisely used the profits from his cleaning company to invest in real estate and a car dealership. This decision to diversify his earnings positioned him to create multiple income streams, which eventually allowed him to build generational wealth. Today, he owns one of the most successful town-car services in the country. While I don't know his company's current ranking, I am confident that it would be high on the list of the top 100 most successful African-American businesses in the country.

Like Bryn, Gregory is another example of an ordinary guy whose self-motivation and discipline opened the doors to extraordinary success in the world of business.

James Robertson is a remarkable example of the power of self-motivation and discipline. At the time of his Detroit Free Press story, James was a 56-year-old man who walked 21 miles one way to work and 21 miles back home every day for five years after his car broke down. He had no choice but to do so because he lacked the funds to replace or repair his car. Despite these unfortunate circumstances, James braved the harsh Michigan winters and walked through some of Detroit's most undesirable neighborhoods. On one occasion, he was even badly beaten.

Nevertheless, James's unwavering self-motivation and discipline are evident in his ability to never miss a day of work or arrive late. This serves as a testament to his remarkable determination. Regardless of the seemingly insurmountable hardships, trials, and tribulations he faced, James Robertson's story demonstrates what a self-motivated and disciplined individual can achieve. He literally put his life on the line every day to overcome obstacles that could have easily defeated him.

Life has a way of eventually rewarding hard work and perseverance. In James's case, the good Lord blessed him with $200,000 in cash, a brand-new car, and several attractive job offers from strangers throughout the state of Michigan. These people heard about his story, I'm sure, just like I did from the Detroit Free Press article written about him, and they respected his perseverance and dedication so much that they felt led by God to bless him with their gifts.

These people heard about his story, I'm sure, just like I did from the Detroit Free Press article written about him. They respected his perseverance and dedication so much that they felt led by God to bless him with their gifts. As cruel as the world can be at times, people admire those who are self-motivated, disciplined, hardworking, and willing to make sacrifices. Let me ask you a question: Can you look at yourself in the mirror and honestly say, "I'm one of those people?" The reason self-motivated, disciplined individuals are able to overcome insurmountable odds is that their "why" is greater than the many reasons to say, "why not quit?" Instead, they answer "why" like this: why? Because it's my decision to succeed. Why? Because it's my right to succeed. And why? Because it's God's will that I succeed. Bryn Forbes is living proof of the rewards that can be realized as a result of self-motivation and discipline. He has carved out a career in the NBA that no one, other than himself, thought was possible.

INTANGIBLE WINNING TRAIT THREE

TALENT HAS TO HAVE PASSION

Tom Izzo, Draymond Green and Magic Johnson

Passion is the straw that stirs the drink. It's the get-up-and-go. It's the wind beneath your wings; without it, you can't fly. I've never seen anything extraordinary accomplished without passion. Frankly speaking, you must be passionate about whatever you endeavor to do in life. It's your passion that is the glue that binds all of your efforts together. It's passion that fuels your motivation. If you don't have it, your work ethic declines and your talent quickly diminishes to nothing.

Passion is a strong, uncontrollable, all-consuming, intense emotion that arouses a person's desire to do their best. There are no better examples of passion in the game of basketball than Spartan legends Mateen Cleaves, Magic Johnson, and Tom Izzo. These guys all project a level of passion so intense that you can feel it throughout the depths of your soul. Whenever you're around them, you can see the passion in their body language and hear it in their voice. No one in the game of basketball has ever played or coached with more passion than these three guys. Whether it's shouting out instructions or screaming words of encouragement, the sound of their voices fills the air with passion. The essence of each guy's passion is uniquely his own and can be easily identified through the individuality of their vocal expression and body language.

Notability Magic's infectious ear-to-ear smile, Mateen's magnificent tongue wag followed by a smile, or Izzo's death-defying scold and fist pump—collectively, each one of these Spartan greats has discovered the unique power of demonstrating outward expressions of passion. They all know how to use passion to fuel the fire of game-winning intensity, energy, and enthusiasm that excites both fans and players alike. Throughout their careers, they have used their expressions of passion to inspire others to commit to a culture of success and winning. The passion it takes to win can never be fake. In fact, to create a championship culture, your passion can only come from a genuine place. The passion that Magic, Mateen, and Izzo possess is real, not just because they're passionate about the game of basketball, but more importantly because they are all genuinely passionate people with agendas greater than merely winning basketball games. Their real passion is about helping other players (people) succeed in the game of life.

Here's a piece of wisdom from me to you: remember this when you're on the road to success — there will be numerous roadblocks, potholes, and narrow passageways. Throughout the civil rights movement, Dr. Martin Luther King, for example, faced some of the tallest barriers and lopsided odds that you could ever imagine. Nevertheless, he was able to overcome those obstacles because he was extraordinarily passionate about changing the world. Today, Dr. King is mostly remembered for his passionate speeches. However, it was not just the content of his speeches that had the greatest impact on his audiences, but also the intense passion with which he spoke every word. Although Dr. King had a clear understanding of how passion impacts success, his journey was not without stumbling blocks. When those stumbling blocks arose, it was his passion that enabled him to persevere and lead a movement that changed the world forever!

In life, we often have a clear vision of our destinations but no idea how to get there. The realization of this can put you in a state of mind that breeds frustration, disappointment, and confusion. Adding to that, you feel completely stuck and at your wit's end. As the outside world starts to play games with your mind, you begin to believe that you're long overdue to reach your destination of success. Consequently, you're at the point of relinquishing any hope you ever had of reaching your desired success. When this happens, if you're not careful, the side effects of pain and doubt will confront you with the most dangerous obstacle blocking you on your road to success: F.E.A.R. (False Evidence Appearing Real). When these detours threaten your progress, you will need the power of passion to refocus your path. It is equally important to realize that although the detours can be frustrating and scary, every time you're forced to take another path, you're getting closer to your final destination of success. In essence, there are no wasted paths, even when fear tells you there is nothing else left that you can do to get to your destination. When you're at that point, it is your passion that will redirect you down the right path to your final destination of success.

Fortunately, every path is often marked with the legacies of people who have walked similar paths to yours. If you're mindful, you can learn from the mistakes and successes of others who have walked similar paths. However, it's your decision to take someone else's path, but that doesn't guarantee that their path will lead you to success or your final destination. What it does mean is that at some point along the way, you're going to have to make your own path.

In the first chapter, "Fundamental # 1 Passing," I discuss how people in the Upper Peninsula (YUPPERS) of Michigan always make their own paths, regardless of the number of walkways available to them. This analogy is why I've always believed that the UP's two most famous native sons, Tom Izzo and Steve Mariucci, had no problem understanding that if they wanted to be successful, they would have to forge their own path to reach that final destination called success. They are both just two ordinary guys, no different from you, doing extraordinary things through the power of passion.

INTANGIBLE WINNING TRAIT FOUR
TALENT HAS TO HAVE INTENSITY,ENERGY &
ENTHUSIASM
LouRawls (Tum Tum) Narin Jr

Regarding winning, achievement, and success, I have never witnessed genuine enthusiasm throughout my entire life that wasn't jump-started by the presence of intensity and energy. Webster's Dictionary defines enthusiasm as "intense energy that brings about eager enjoyment, interest, and approval." Notice that the definition begins by using the words "intense" and "energy" to describe enthusiasm. I believe another word that should be added to the definition of enthusiasm is "genuine."

Tum-Tum LouRawls Nairn Jr. holds a special place in the hearts and minds of Spartan Nation because of his commitment to playing every game with intensity, energy, and enthusiasm. If you ever had the opportunity to be around Tum, you would quickly realize that he approaches every day of his life with enthusiasm.

LouRawls Nairn Jr., better known as "Tum Tum," has a captivating story. It's a story that inspires, motivates, and empowers people from every walk of life. Before deciding to leave home at the tender age of 13 and pursue a better life for himself and his family, he grew up in the hoods of Nassau, Bahamas. His decision to leave home would ultimately change the quality of his life forever. However, he wouldn't get to enjoy the rewards of his decision until his life's journey hit him with numerous hardships, trials, and tribulations. It was only through his unrelenting persistence, determination, and sheer G.U.T.S. (Glory Under Tough Situations) that he was able to overcome the consequences of those hardships, trials, and tribulations. In spite of his difficulties, he went on to eventually earn a basketball scholarship to play at Michigan State University.

Tum's entire being notably represents the following three intangible winning traits: intensity, energy, and enthusiasm. All three of these traits are essential factors if you want to sustain and maintain persistence, discipline, perseverance, and the guts needed to keep you from eventually quitting on your dreams over an extended period of time. These traits give us the strength to make it through the daily grind associated with the work it takes to overcome life's hardships, trials, and tribulations. Of the three traits, Tum is the embodiment of enthusiasm, a trait that is only as effective as the optimal genuine intensity and energy that fosters its presence.

A lot of non-energetic players/people try to fake enthusiasm, but their body language always gives them away. The game of basketball is a good example of how coaches and fans can quickly sniff out players and teams that lack enthusiasm. The blank, emotionless facial expressions, the non-energetic hand claps, and lifeless body movements all characterize a player's lack of intensity, energy, and enthusiasm.

Our coaching staff at Michigan State has always adhered to the philosophy of recruiting players who possess three essential qualities: 1) *talent*, 2) *intensity* and *energy*, and 3) *enthusiasm*. We have a special term for these types of players: OKG's, which stands for *Our Kinda Guys*. This label serves two purposes: One, it signifies that they align with the characteristics we seek in a Spartan basketball player, and secondly, it recognizes the fact that we cannot achieve consistent *High Performance Maximum Xecution* without players who bring intensity, energy, and enthusiasm to the team. Through past experiences, we have learned that players with these traits, like Tum, can contribute to winning games for our team even without scoring a single point.

They're capable of changing the course of a game just through their enthusiasm alone, particularly when things aren't going well. Throughout Tum's career, we would put him in the game whenever our team needed a boost to get us going. We knew that it was in those moments that his enthusiasm would be most beneficial in enhancing our team's chances to win. Whenever Tum got off the bench to go into the game, it wasn't a cool and casual walk to check in at the scorer's table. Rather, he would bounce off the bench and run to the scorer's table like a thoroughbred ready to be let out of the gate at the start of a horse race. Once he was on the court, every player and fan in the entire arena could feel the full effects of his intensity, energy, and enthusiasm. He was well known for slapping the floor while at the same time motioning to the crowd to help lift our team's energy. It was common to see him wave his arms, put on an ear-to-ear smile, then get into a death-defying defensive stance and yell, "Let's go!" His intensity, energy, and enthusiasm demonstrate why year after year we manage to win two or three games we truly should have lost.

It's a well-known fact that our program draws on the abilities of players like Tum and Travis Walton, who know how to use intensity, energy, and enthusiasm to get our team to play at a high-performance maximum Xecution level. They both understand that winning requires playing at a higher intensity level than your opponents. Consequently, over the years, we have beaten teams that were more talented than us simply because of our intensity, energy, and enthusiasm.

One of the most overlooked secrets to Tom Izzo's success as a coach is his ability to consistently get his teams to play with intensity, energy, and enthusiasm. One of Tom's superpowers is his ability to read body language. He frequently uses this superpower to assess the mentality of his team. He does this because he knows that good body language is an important aspect of good leadership that brings about intensity, energy, and enthusiasm.

He believes that poor body language is the single most detrimental factor to a team's level of energy, intensity, enthusiasm, and ultimately its overall performance. On the other hand, he believes that good body language, especially if embraced and demonstrated daily by your best players, will enhance the entire team's level of energy, intensity, enthusiasm, as well as its overall ability to play at a high-performance maximum Xecution level. He understands that unfortunately, your best players aren't always good leaders and don't always demonstrate the necessary good body language required to be a high-performance maximum Xecution team. However, the winningest players always show great body language, which is why they are not only the best players but also great winners. The development of good body language is one of the first things Tom instills in all of his players, particularly if they don't already have it. But it's something he definitely demands from his best players and coaching staff.

Tom believes, like most coaches, that his teams should always practice the same way they play in games. However, he is different from most other coaches because he believes in

122

practicing with intensity, energy, and enthusiasm every day. Tom stands apart from his fellow coaches by considering intensity, energy, and enthusiasm as skills that need to be practiced daily, just like basic basketball skills such as dribbling, passing, or shooting. In fact, he adamantly believes that a team cannot consistently play with intensity, energy, and enthusiasm in games if these qualities are not emphasized during practice every day.

The following statement describes how Kristin Ray, one of our administrative staff members, described the unmistakable sign that practice was about to begin: "Every day, we knew practice was about to start when we heard the deafening, intense screams of Tom's voice echoing up to the office from the practice gym below. He would shout words of encouragement to his teammates in a fun but serious manner, getting them fired up before practice."

Generally, our practice starts with some form of stretching and warm-up exercises. However, that time is never an excuse to lack energy. Tum always leads the warm-ups while encouraging his teammates to chant, clap, and dance to the rhythm of the music playing during the warm-up. If you were to interview any of our players, they would tell you that there was never a day when Tum wasn't full of intensity, energy, and enthusiasm. His ability to inject intensity, energy, and enthusiasm into his teammates made it second nature for our team to have the same high-level intensity, energy, and enthusiasm every single day, whether it was practice or games.

This same intensity, energy, and enthusiasm can turn a low-performing average basketball team into a high-performance maximum Xecution team. They are the same winning traits that will make you a high-performance maximum Xecution player in the game of life.

The Phoenix Suns of the NBA recognized Tum's enthusiastic approach to life as a characteristic they wanted to establish within their team. Shortly after his graduation from Michigan State, the Suns immediately hired Tum as a team leader, a position that had never existed in the NBA until the Suns hired him in 2018. His job description was simply to help them build a culture of intensity, energy, and enthusiasm, just like he had done for our teams at Michigan State. When they were considering Tum for the job, the Vice President of the team called Chief to talk about Tum. The call caught Chief completely off guard because he initially thought they were calling to discuss Tum as a prospective player for their team. The reason the call was particularly puzzling to Chief was that the caller's first question was, "What can you tell me about Tum?" This question is commonly asked when NBA teams have a genuine interest in a player as a potential draft pick.

However, the caller quickly acknowledged his real reason for calling. At that point, Chief not only recommended Tum for the job but also sold the caller on Tum's suitability for the position. The Suns organization was so impressed with Tum's ability to foster a culture of intensity, energy, and enthusiasm that they considered him for a role to do the same for their entire franchise. Tum embodies the epitome of intensity and energy, the essential characteristics that ignite the fuel and ignite a person's internal flame of enthusiasm.

INTANGIBLE WINNING TRAIT FIVE

TALENT HAS TO BE CONFIDENT AND HAVE COMPETITIVE DRIVE

Miles Bridges

Miles Bridges grew up in Flint, Michigan, a town once renowned for its car production and professional athletes, long before the recent water crisis. In fact, Sports Illustrated once published an article depicting Flint as a city with the highest number of professional athletes per capita in the entire United States. During its prime, Flint's inhabitants, like those of most urban industrial cities, were tough, blue-collar, confident, and highly competitive. Consequently, the athletes from Flint shared the same mentality as the town's residents. Although Miles did not grow up during the city's era of economic and athletic prosperity, the Flint town mentality that fostered great athletes somehow managed to become ingrained in his DNA. I believe this development can be attributed to a few distinguishing factors. First and foremost, his father, Raymond Bridges, was an exceptional athlete in both football and basketball and was a member of the 1972 Flint Northern State Championship basketball team. Secondly, despite the city's economic hardships reducing the number of outstanding elite athletes, the voices of those in the community who were part of its legendary athletic past have not been silenced.

The stories of that era have been etched into the hearts and minds of the young people growing up there even today, stories told by men and women who actually participated in and witnessed the era during its glory. These stories have been priceless to young athletes like Miles, who have dreamed of one day playing basketball professionally.

In my estimation, Miles was able to develop the same confidence and competitive edge as the great Flint town players of the past, even without ever experiencing a day playing in the city's legendary era. He achieved this by listening to and learning from the stories he heard while growing up. At a young age, Miles made a decision that would forever change the course of his life, a decision that most guys wouldn't have dared to make because they wouldn't have had the confidence and competitive drive required to leave home and compete against the best high school players in the country on a daily basis.

Miles' greatest moment as a Spartan demonstrated both confidence and a competitive drive during our 2018 Big Ten Championship game against Purdue, in which he hit the game-winning shot. He made that shot in his last home game as a Spartan, playing on the Breslin Center floor in front of a packed house, with the championship on the line. The mental toughness, confidence, and competitive drive it took for him to attempt and make that shot in his final game as a Spartan clearly demonstrated his unwavering confidence and competitive drive. He hit the shot despite struggling to make shots throughout the game.

Before Miles hit the shot, Tom called a timeout to set up a play for a good shot. I know for a fact that Tom initially didn't intend to set up the play for Miles to take the shot because he hadn't been shooting well throughout the game. However, what changed his mind was the confidence with which Miles assured everybody that he would hit the shot if they got him the ball. I clearly remember his body language and what he was saying as he walked from the playing floor to our huddle. When he finally reached the huddle, he kept repeating what he had been saying while walking off the floor: "Get me the ball, I'm going to hit the shot."

Once Tom had drawn up the play and our guys broke the huddle to return to the floor, Miles walked to the end of our bench and motioned for Tum Tum Nairns to come toward him. When they were finally face to face, he hugged Tum, and I heard him say, "I'm going to hit this shot just for you." He knew fully well that Tum was a senior and he wanted to send him out as a champion in his last home game. He then proceeded to walk out onto the floor and did exactly what he said he would do: he hit the shot.

Throughout my entire coaching career, I've witnessed highly talented college players who failed to reach their potential due to a lack of confidence and competitive drive. Confidence and competitive drive are closely intertwined. Honestly, I cannot recall coaching a player who lacked confidence but possessed competitive drive simultaneously. I've come across many "3 o'clock shooters" - players who display confidence in shooting during practice sessions but struggle to shoot with the same level of confidence in a game. Let's delve into the mindset behind why the most successful basketball players have a high degree of confidence. The reason is simple: the majority of them openly acknowledge that their confidence is a direct outcome of the countless hours they have invested day after day, month after month, year after year, diligently honing their shooting skills from morning, noon and night.

What you'll find with most of these high-performance individuals is a unique characteristic common to many of them: the majority of them believe that their confidence was developed while working on their shot alone, by themselves, without the supervision or motivation of a trainer or coach. They also believe that their hard work has earned them the right to be confident, and in turn, their confidence reinforces their belief that they can make shots from anywhere at any time, from any spot on the basketball court. This includes hitting free throws under pressure and making game-winning shots during games. These players are what I call "know guys." I call them this because they never second-guess their ability to make shots; they know they can! Why? Because of their hard work, they believe that they've earned the right to know, which justifies their right to be super confident.

However, most confident and competitively driven players realize that it's important to maintain a realistic perspective of their confidence, because as true competitors, they know that confidence can distort their thinking with ego-driven thoughts. For example, they might think, "I don't need to continue doing extra work because nobody is better than me." This way of thinking is toxic to maintaining the edge that makes elite players champions.

The reason this toxic way of thinking never crosses the mind of competitively driven elite players is because they know it can lead to the demise of their career. In fact, players who have reached the elite level of play usually have such high expectations of themselves that they tend to have the opposite mindset. Players with a competitively driven mindset are always thinking about how they can continuously improve. They are constantly on the lookout for what their competition is doing to make themselves better. The reason for wanting to know what their competitors are doing is because they are well aware that their competitors are willing to do whatever it takes to beat them.

Furthermore, he knows that he has to work even harder, smarter, and more intensely if he wants to continue to beat his competition. Yet, as a competitively driven player, he confidently seeks out his competition and looks forward to the day when he will be able to match his skills against his most formidable competitor in battle. The all-time great quarterback, Tom Brady, clearly illustrates the mindset of an elite, confident, competitively driven player when he said this regarding competition: "If you're going to compete against me, you better be ready to give up your life because I've already given up mine." Without question, he made this statement to convey that if his competition wants to beat him, they must be willing to push themselves beyond all physical and mental limitations, even to the point of near death. That's why he is a 14-time Pro-Bowler and a 6-time Super Bowl Champion. Win, lose, or draw, a true competitor never backs away from competition or the challenges associated with winning. The competitor never thinks in terms of losing because they are confident in the overall body of work they have put into preparing themselves to succeed against all odds.

The world is full of talented people who really don't know what it means to compete. Their mindset is not one that is willing to risk life and limb to succeed. Generally speaking, they think this way because they confuse hard work with competing. They've never been told or taken the time to figure out that the two are not the same. To compete, you must be willing to work as hard or harder than your competitors. Additionally, non-competitive players or people don't understand that there is a difference between losing and getting beaten. Charlie Cole, a good friend, mentor, and one of the most unheralded college basketball coaches in the history of the game, once said something to me that was not only a profound statement in terms of the game of basketball but also one of the most profound statements I've ever heard about the game of life. His statement was simply this: "More games are lost than won." In other words, competitively driven players or people never lose, but they do get beaten.

Why? Because of the following three things: 1) they're *confident* they can *win*, 2) they're prepared to *win*, and 3) they're willing to put forth and maintain a level of effort that matches or exceeds the level of effort their opponent is willing to give throughout the duration of their competition. On the other hand, *non-competitive* players lose because 1) they beat themselves, 2) they're not confident they can *win*, and 3) they're not prepared and unwilling to put forth the effort needed to beat their competition. These factors essentially determine if your measure of *talent* can consistently allow you to play at a level of *High Performance Maximum Xecution* because you've done the necessary work it takes to be *confident* and *competitively driven*.

INTANGIBLE WINNING TRAIT SIX

TALENT HAS TO HAVE GOOD LEADERSHIP

"Leadership Has To Be Willing To Confront and Demand"

Draymond (DayDay) Green & Travis Walton

Draymond Green, both as a college player at Michigan State and now as a professional player with the Golden State Warriors, is a great example of how leadership affects the performance of talented teammates. Throughout his career, his leadership qualities have allowed him to have a significant impact on the most talented players on his teams. An incident during his time at Michigan State serves as evidence of his leadership abilities. One day during practice, while shooting free throws, Draymond's teammate Derrick Nix unexpectedly punched him. Chief immediately expelled Nix from practice, which was a rightful response, and even considered removing him from the team permanently. However, Draymond, as the leader of our team, took matters into his own hands. Despite any anger, frustration, or humiliation he may have felt, a few minutes after the incident, Draymond went down to the locker room and brought Nix back up to continue practicing.

He did this because it was his senior year, and he knew we needed Nix's talent if we were going to win a championship. That's how obsessed he was with winning, and he's still that way right now as the team leader of the Golden State Warriors. Draymond could have demanded that Chief kick Nix off the team, and he would have done it. But because Tom knew that Draymond was the type of leader who was not afraid to confront and demand that his teammates play at a high-performance maximum Xecution level, he trusted Draymond's decision to keep Nix on the team. As an effective leader, Draymond used the situation to help him encourage one of the team's most talented players to be a better teammate. He could have escalated the situation by throwing a punch back or acting like a crazed madman, which he had every right to do, but rather he decided to use the situation to his advantage.

However, his thought process was that it was better for him to swallow his pride and do what was best for our team. As it turned out, the situation became a defining moment in Derrick Nix's life for several reasons. First, it gave him an opportunity to learn valuable life lessons regarding how to handle confrontations without resorting to violence. Second, he realized that Draymond, as the team's leader, would hold him accountable for his actions,

130

and there would be consequences if his actions were detrimental to the team. Finally, he understood that it didn't matter whether he was the most talented player or the least talented player on the team; he would be held accountable for demonstrating negative behavior. Draymond was determined not to let Nix's negative behavior break the fabric of our team's culture.

He was able to make an impact on Nix that raised his level of respect for Draymond from zero to one hundred immediately. Draymond knew what Derrick could do and how much our team could benefit from his talent. His decision to insist that Derrick stay on the team not only made us a better team but also exhibited extraordinary selfless leadership on his part.

If *talent* is going to successfully perform at a *level of High Performance Maximum Xecution*, it has to have *effective leadership* to be able to do it consistently. The only way to make that happen is for *leadership* to be willing to hold *talent accountable* for performing at a *High Performance Maximum Xecution Level* every day. It is the job of *effective leadership* to always make sure that it's profoundly apparent to every individual, the team, or organization that *talent alone is never enough.*

The great Chicago Bulls teams of the 80s were led by Michael Jordan and Scottie Pippen. These two guys not only talked the talk, but they also walked the walk, or better put, they "worked the work." As the *leaders* of the team, they set the standards of *accountability* that their teammates would be held to by first holding themselves *accountable*. The following is a great example of what they did to set the standard of how hard they expected their teammates to work every day.

The following is what they did daily; the two of them would get to the gym every day, two hours before practice, and play full court one-on-one to get their point across to their teammates.

Afterwards, they would practice as hard as the rest of their teammates during the regular practice session that same day, without any rest before the start of practice. Think about the message that it sent to the rest of the team regarding how hard they would be expected to work every day. Michael and Scotty were not interested in just showing up and going through the motions. They wanted to win championships, and to do that, they knew their teammates would have to play at a high-performance maximum Xecution level every day. The two of them also realized that it would be their job as team leaders to hold their teammates accountable to a high-performance maximum Xecution championship level at all times, whether that be in practice or games. Consequently, because of their effective leadership qualities, they were able to win six NBA championships.

Scotty and Michael deserve commendation for their efforts in holding their teammates accountable. However, it is unfortunate that their efforts reveal a shameful truth about most talented individuals. Once they embark on the path to success, they encounter challenges that convince them that their talent alone is insufficient. Most talented individuals are unwilling to hold themselves accountable unless they receive guidance and support from effective leadership, which pushes them to perform at their highest level every day.

The period spanning from 1998 to 2000 is widely regarded as the greatest era in the history of basketball at Michigan State. Notable achievements during this time include four consecutive Big Ten championships, a national championship in 2000, and three consecutive appearances in the Final Four. In 2002, Tom noticed that everyone in our program had become complacent and content. This prompted Brian Gregory, one of our assistant coaches at the time (currently the head coach at South Florida), to coin a memorable quote: "Championship effort is the only effort accepted here."

Tom, with his effective leadership and commitment to holding everyone accountable, swiftly ordered the quote to be displayed throughout our entire facility. Looking back, it was Tom's actions that prevented what could have been a disastrous season.

When talking about Spartan Basketball, one of the most argumentative discussions over the years has been the subject of *leadership*. The ongoing debate among Spartan Nation for years has centered around who is the best leader in the history of Michigan State basketball. Whenever the debate comes up, the three names that are always at the forefront of the conversation are Magic Johnson, Mateen Cleaves, and Travis Walton. Of course, the accolades of Magic and Mateen speak for themselves, most notably the national championships they both won — Magic in 1979 and Mateen in 2000.

However, although Travis Walton's career wasn't capped off with a national championship like the other two great leaders before him, he is still considered by many Michigan State basketball enthusiasts to be the best leader to ever wear a Spartan basketball uniform. Many of them believe that if you exclude basketball talent and base the argument solely on leadership skills, Travis Walton comes out on top. Personally, I think it's impossible to definitively determine who the best leader is because there are so many immeasurable factors to consider that are connected to each player's career. I don't believe anyone could make a reasonable case for either individual. Nevertheless, supporters of Travis often highlight the fact that he was not the best player on his team as a justification for why he should hold the leadership crown.

As I mentioned earlier, talent requires strong leadership to consistently perform at a high-performance level. This is because most players, even the most talented ones, lack the self-motivation and discipline necessary to meet the demands of achieving peak performance every day. Because Travis understood this, here's what he did to assure his team's success.

1. He consistently prioritized the team.
2. He was the most accomplished winner on the team.
3. He fostered meaningful relationships with every player.
4. He fearlessly confronted challenges and demanded excellence.

The following story demonstrates the impact and power of Travis Walton's leadership. In 2009, we had to beat Louisville in the Midwest Regional Championship Game to get to the Final Four. At that time, they were the number one team in the nation and predicted to win the national championship that year. I'm a big believer that most games are won before the teams ever hit the floor. Our 7 AM walkthrough on the morning of our game with Louisville confirmed my belief. Normally, we go to the gym for our walkthrough, which typically takes about an hour to complete. But because we were playing a noon game, we decided to have our walkthrough that morning in the hotel ballroom. I always got the players up in the morning before breakfast or early morning film, whichever Chief would decide to do first whenever we were in a hotel on the road.

But that particular morning, by the time I got to their rooms, they were already up and in the ballroom, ready to go. The players were so focused and proficient that Chief ended the walkthrough before I could get downstairs to the ballroom. The walkthrough that morning couldn't have lasted more than 15 minutes. Later, I found out that the night before our walkthrough, Travis called a meeting in his room and *demanded* that every player know the scouting report on Louisville inside and out. He then adamantly expressed to the team that he wanted the walkthrough to be mistake-free, high intensity, high energy, and bubbling with enthusiasm. He made sure that every player understood that if the walkthrough wasn't the way he explained it should be, there was going to be a *confrontation* between him and anyone who showed up to the walkthrough unprepared and unenthusiastic, and he made sure that they understood that the *confrontation* wasn't going to be pretty.

The reason for Travis's effectiveness as a leader was his ability to utilize relationship-driven leadership to build meaningful, genuine relationships with all of his teammates. Clearly, it was the relationships with his teammates that gave him a license to confront and demand that they consistently play at a high-performance, maximum Xecution level, regardless of circumstances. That day, because of Travis's outstanding leadership, we went on to win the Midwest Regional Championship and an opportunity to play in the 2009 Final Four in front of our hometown fans in Detroit.

Travis Walton was born and raised in Lima, Ohio, a small town with a rich tradition of basketball and quality players. Although we felt that Travis was good enough to play for us, it wasn't his basketball skills that most intrigued us about him. When we watched him play, we could clearly see he had both the toughness and leadership qualities that we so desperately needed to make our team special.

Today, it doesn't surprise me that Travis is one of the best skill trainers in the basketball profession. He is the personal trainer for Draymond Green and several other NBA and college players. However, it has always been his dream to be a coach in the NBA or college. After he exhausted his eligibility he came back to school to finish his degree and work for us as a student assistant to assure that he would be able to fulfill his dream of one day becoming a coach once his playing career was over. Unfortunately just as his coaching career was on the up swing he was falsely accused of something he did not do. He was immediately let go by the NBA team he was working for at the time, even before having his day in court to prove his innocence.

The false accusations have seemingly ruined his chances of ever coaching in the NBA or college. Here's a young man who is a *High Performance, Maximum Xecution,* relationship-driven leader, very capable of being a great coach, and has done everything the right way. However, no one will give him a chance to resume his career as a coach because of a false accusation. I just hope that a quality basketball organization somewhere out there in the near future, in need of a high-performance, maximum Xecution, relationship-driven leader, will give Travis a chance to once again have the opportunity to fulfill his dream, which he so deservingly deserves.

INTANGIBLE WINNING TRAIT SEVEN

TALENT HAS TO HAVE G.U.T.S,

Quentin, Simone & Michael Ray Garland

The word "guts" is often used to describe the toughness, tenacity, and inner will of an individual. The acronym G.U.T.S. stands for "*Glory Under Tough Situations*," accurately characterizing the content of this chapter. I specifically chose the word "under" instead of "in" because being in a tough situation is much different from being under a tough situation. Let me clarify my thoughts: typically, when you hear the word "under" used to describe a person's situation, it's usually not very good. For example, "He was under the influence of alcohol," "He will be under for twelve hours during surgery," "He's under investigation." To be straightforward, situations referred to as "under" are usually critical and require G.U.T.S. to emerge victorious from them.

Most situations involve overcoming overwhelming odds of some sort. I don't know of many successful people in the game of basketball or life who have not had to overcome a number of such situations before reaching the pinnacle of their success. Unfortunately, all too often, these situations appear unexpectedly, in multiples, and at the most inconvenient times in your life. The courage it takes to perform heroic feats in a basketball game is the same courage that helps you navigate through the difficulties of these situations. Difficulties are generally the result of some underlying situation and can become distractions that hinder your opportunity to succeed. However, it's important to realize that they are part of the challenges you face as you pursue success throughout your life's journey. Once you've worked through those challenges, the game of life recognizes that you have the courage to fight through the difficult challenges associated with these situations.

At that point, life seems to open the door to success as a reward for having the G.U.T.S. to press forward despite facing life's most difficult challenges while still pursuing your dreams. If you think that talent alone will get you through life's tough challenges, you are gravely mistaken and will never have the chance to reach the level of success you seek. It takes more than talent to exert the necessary mental and physical willpower needed to succeed. Talent alone won't guarantee you enough willpower to be successful, but having G.U.T.S. will. I'm talking about the type of willpower it takes to meet the demands associated with having the guts to grind every day at a high-performance maximum Xecution level. The willpower to continually outwork, outcompete, and never relent under any circumstances, difficulties, or challenges. Believe me, talent alone won't push you through the everyday grind it takes to surpass the willpower of your competitors. However, your G.U.T.S. will ignite a competitive spirit within you that will empower you to overcome the challenges of difficult situations.

It has always troubled me as well; it has been hard for me to understand how a guy can overcome challenging situations in the game of basketball but can't, or better yet won't, do what's necessary to overcome similar situations in the game of life. I'm talking about the same guys who weren't afraid to take the last shot or hit the game-winning free throws throughout their entire basketball careers. Yet once they're done playing, they struggle to translate how to use the same G.U.T.S. to overcome challenging situations in the game of life. We have all heard the disturbing stories about these same kinds of guys who were outstanding players throughout their careers.

We are all aware of guys who made a lot of money, blew it all, and are now broke. However, I'm not really referring to those guys. They have a completely different story. The guys I'm talking about are the millions of former players who were talented in high school but didn't quite make it to college ball. They were prominent college players but only had brief professional careers because they weren't good enough to stick in the pros. All of these guys are no different from the millions of people in the game of life who have what it takes to be highly successful but, in many cases, can barely make ends meet. These guys, for some reason, don't understand that the same thoughts and strategies that made them successful in the game of basketball are the same thoughts and strategies that can make them just as successful in the game of life.

Mat Ishbia, a walk-on player on our 2000 national championship team, is one of the best examples of a basketball player who used my seven intangible winning traits: hard work, self-motivation & discipline, passion, intensity, energy & enthusiasm, leadership, confidence & competitive drive, and G.U.T.S., to build a Fortune 500 company. He told me that during the process of building his company, he faced numerous insurmountable obstacles, and it was only his G.U.T.S. and his understanding of the other six intangible winning traits that he learned as a player at Michigan State that got him through those tough times. As a result, he has built a company that has estimated earnings of 5.1 billion dollars a year. Before his rise to the top of the business world, his most notable accomplishments were being a member of our 2000 National Championship team and the play he instructed our staff to run during our national championship game, which led to us scoring a much-needed basket at a critical time against Florida.

Today, he is the owner and President of United Wholesale Mortgages (UWM), the number one wholesale commercial real estate mortgage company in the country. In fact, his company has recently been named the top mortgage company in the country for the third consecutive year, earning the title in 2022. When he assumed control of the company, it ranked 257th out of 300 similar companies in the United States and was the least profitable among his father's various business ventures. Despite lacking prior experience in the lending industry, I offered him a position as an assistant coach on my staff at Cleveland State before he embarked on his career in lending. Although he seriously considered the offer, his father Jeff Ishbia rightfully advised him against accepting the coaching position. Another noteworthy detail about Mat's father, Jeff, who is an attorney, is that he represented our star freshman forward, Jason Richardson, when the NCAA erroneously declared him ineligible to play. Thanks to Jeff's efforts, Jason's eligibility was ultimately reinstated.

Once Mat turned down my job offer, he gave himself six months after his graduation from Michigan State to see if he would have any interest in sticking with it. At the end of the six months, he discovered he loved it. He then continued to work in the company while learning everything he could about the business for the next six years. At the end of the sixth year, he took over the company as President and CEO.

Mat attributes his ability to move his company quickly from worst to first not to his ability to make savvy business decisions like many of his competitors' CEOs, but rather to his focus on the seven intangible winning traits that are characteristic of all successful people, regardless of their occupation, life desires, or dreams. He went on to say, without reservation, that he learned both the power and value of these seven traits while playing basketball for us at Michigan State. Mat said that he knew that if he stuck with these intangible winning traits, he would eventually turn his company into a high-performance maximum Xecution level team that would surpass his competition.

What he said to me next resonated deep within my soul and once again confirmed my ambition as to why I needed to write this book. He said, "Coach, I wish more of my teammates who no longer play basketball would take advantage of what you guys taught us," referring to the seven intangible winning traits. I said, "Mat, you're right. Thank you for having the guts to tell me what I needed to hear.

The quote "God works in mysterious ways" is a perfect description of the life challenges faced by each of my children. My youngest son, Michael Ray, gave me the G.U.T.S. acronym after going through his own trying situations due to heart issues that nearly took his life. His story exemplifies courage, inner depth, and resolve, which are the qualities represented by G.U.T.S. in triumphing over dire, life-threatening situations.

The health issue that almost brought his life to an untimely demise is a heart condition known as cardiomyopathy, specifically heart failure, which resulted in several critical complications. Among his three surgeries in a month, the most life-threatening was a procedure that had never been done before in the history of modern medicine. This procedure was necessary because his heart pump, called an LVAD, was causing infection in his heart. They had to find a solution to keep him alive until he could receive a donor's heart for a transplant.

The procedure was so complicated that his surgeon, Dr. Wise, and a hundred and one other surgeons from all over the world worked together with him to devise a plan that would take twelve hours of surgery to implement. Praise God, the surgery was successful, and eight days later, on June 1st, he was blessed with a heart for transplant. To this day, I thank God, the doctors, and nurses at the Cleveland Clinic, and most of all, my son Michael Ray, for having the G.U.T.S. to push through his dismal circumstances and remain here with me in the land of the living. Ray isn't the only one of my three children to go through life-changing circumstances. I get emotional every time I think about the trauma, heartbreak, and fear that they each had to endure at certain times in their lives to overcome their difficult situations.

My daughter Simone has been a survivor her entire life. She faced a challenge at the early age of 3 when she was diagnosed with a life-threatening disease known as Kawasaki. At that time, she was the third known case of it in the country. Kawasaki can be fatal if not properly diagnosed and treated. By the grace of God, her pediatrician, Dr. Weinblatt, was the only doctor in the country who successfully diagnosed and treated the disease. Although she fully recovered from the life-threatening ramifications of the disease, it left her with side effects that affected her brain's ability to process information in a normal manner. This condition presented her with challenges. Later on, we discovered that the majority of people with her condition are never able to function normally throughout their entire life. The most troubling part of this was that my wife and I were not aware of her condition until she was a young adult already attending college.

However, we were amazed when we found out from the psychologist, who finally diagnosed her condition, that she should never have been able to learn to read and write, let alone make it through high school. He went on to say that most people with her condition normally don't graduate from high school, let alone attend college. His explanation of the consequences of her condition prompted us to ask him a very provocative question. We asked him to tell us how she could have possibly counteracted the ill effects of her condition without any

141

professional help as a child. His answer was plain and simple: *"it was her will."* My first thought was, "Wow, I've just spent the past twenty years of my life living with my daughter without realizing that she was one of the most incredible individuals I've ever met." It was her guts that enabled her to willfully surpass her brain's inability to adequately process information and overcome insurmountable odds to achieve what the world said she couldn't, despite what was thought to be cognitively impossible.

Again, I want to take this opportunity to thank God, Dr. Weinblatt, and most of all my daughter Simone for having the G.U.T.S. to fight with every ounce of her being and the willful determination to continually accomplish things in her life that should have been impossible. Simone, for that reason, babe, I want you to know that I love you and that you have been an inspiration to me more than you'll ever know.

Finally, I want to recognize my first-born child, Quentin, as a great husband, father, and advocate for those who don't have a voice themselves. He has had a desire to help the disenfranchised long before the current focus on social injustice issues. My wife, Cynthia, and I had him when we were 19 and 22-year-old college students at Northern Michigan University. During his toddler years, our time at Northern played a significant role in his intellectual development. From the moment we brought him home from Marquette General Hospital, he became the campus baby. We never had to worry about a babysitter because nearly everyone on campus wanted to spend time with him. He started reading at the age of three because he was exposed daily to the proper rudiments of learning before he could even talk and walk. Cynthia and I can't take full credit for his intellectual development because there were a number of friends who lovingly poured into him as a child. As a result, he's intellectually gifted and uses his abilities to research professional development strategies that help disenfranchised individuals build the skills needed to advance their careers professionally.

He's like me in many ways, but our most common characteristic is our shared love for teaching. Currently, he resides in Atlanta with his wife and two boys. Prior to that, he lived in Cleveland, OH, where he experienced some hard times because he couldn't find a job that paid him enough to afford both a car and an apartment at the same time. Those years turned out to be some of the most challenging episodes in his life. It all started when his only means of transportation was a broken-down bike with only one pedal, which he rode to work every day because he couldn't afford to repair or replace his car. Additionally, he couldn't even afford the daily cost of bus fare to commute to and from work.

Determined not to lose his job he made a decision that tested his G.U.T.S. each and everyday. A decision that put him in harms way everyday just to get to work. I always knew he was a pretty tough kid but I didn't realize the measure of his toughness until I saw that he was willing to literally put his life on the line in an effort to get to work every day for nearly a year. The route he had to take everyday took him through East Cleveland, one of the city's most notoriously dangerous neighborhoods. I thank the Lord even now for protecting him from any bodily hurt, harm or danger as he traveled the streets of East Cleveland on those early dark mornings riding his bike through one of Cleveland's most treacherous neighborhoods in order to get to work everyday.

In hindsight, the odds were overwhelmingly in favor of him getting hit by a car, beaten up, or shot and killed for no reason other than trying to get to work in an area known for such incidents regularly. Son, I know that you've always done things to try to make me proud, but I don't think you realize that I've been proud of you from the day you were born and I first held you in my arms as a twenty-two-year-old father of his first born!!!

Remember this, if you don't remember anything else in this chapter; *talent without G.U.T.S. is useless.*

CHAPTER THREE

Characteristic #3 – Coachable

Mike (OG) Garland Draymond (DayDay) Green

One of Tom Izzo's favorite quotes is," Listen to learn and learn to listen;" In other words, your ability to learn confirms your willingness to effectively listen and follow instructions. The best coaches in the game of basketball know how to effectively communicate instruction. The most successful players(people) in the game of basketball as well as life are commonly effective listeners. As a result, in the game of basketball we refer to them as coachable because their willingness to listen makes them *coachable*. The love-hate relationship between players and their *Coaches* is critical because the *Coach* has to always honestly evaluate the player, without being afraid of telling him exactly what he needs to hear. It's not a secret that most players don't like criticism, but the great players accept it willingly. Their willingness to accept criticism greatly enhances their chance to develop an elite level of *High Performance Maximum Xecution* play.

My first coach was a 16-year-old teenager named Mike Jones. He gave me my first opportunity to play organized ball when he invited me to play on his neighborhood sandlot baseball and football teams. Today, Mike is a minister, which doesn't surprise me because even back then he had a ministering heart. I owe my love of sports to Mike because, during my formative years, his influence introduced me to the world of sports. The love for sports effectively changed the course of my life. Today, I live a quality of life I never dreamed possible because of the sport of basketball. Thank you, Mike, for the seeds of success you so lovingly sowed into me during my formative years.

Whatever your particular endeavor in life may be, it's incredibly important that you have a coach or mentor who is an expert in your particular field. Whoever that person turns out to be, he or she has to be willing to tell you what you need to hear rather than what you want to hear. If your coach or mentor only tells you how great you are and is never willing to confront you about your weaknesses. Get rid of him as soon as possible because you'll never reach your full potential as a player. However, your attitude towards coaching plays a significant role in how much a mentor can help you become a better person. If you're willing to be coachable, it means you must be open to accepting criticism from your mentor in order to grow from your experiences, rather than just going through them. This may sound easy, but most players have a hard time accepting constructive criticism, as they perceive it as a personal attack. Consequently, players who are not coachable tend to lack discipline and self-motivation, and they require a skilled coach who can effectively utilize constructive confrontation to help them improve. Tom Izzo, for example, frequently employs constructive confrontation as a technique to teach his players the importance of intense preparation and hard work. He is never satisfied with the performance of his players, particularly his best players. He is constantly evaluating them to find things to criticize them about, which will ultimately make them better players. Another reason he is critical of his best players is to prevent them from developing an inflated ego. An inflated ego is a character flaw that makes them susceptible to complacency, which ultimately hinders their performance. Both Tom and I probably pushed Cassius Winston, Mateen Cleaves, and Morris Peterson harder than any of our past players because we knew their potential and wanted to ensure they reached their full potential.

The following story about Draymond Green depicts precisely how coachability relates to success. When Draymond was a freshman, he was not the basketball player you know him as today. Regardless of his flaws, Tom Izzo saw something special in him that others did not see. What he saw in Draymond was a kid whom he could eventually mold into a great player. He saw a highly intelligent young man with a basketball IQ that was off the charts, along with the mental and physical toughness it takes to be an elite player. Chief was just as aware that Draymond had a lot of work to do before he would become the player he envisioned. In fact, Draymond was overweight, out of shape, and opposed to any sort of constructive criticism. However, Chief realized, all things considered, that he would have to first develop a relationship of trust with Draymond if he was going to convince him to fully commit to being coachable and accepting of the constructive criticism that would turn him into an elite player.

Along those lines, in April of 2015, I decided to do something about my weight and fitness. At the time, I weighed 249 pounds. Once I started, I was able to reach 218 pounds by November of that same year. Although 218 was close to what my doctor recommended, I struggled to reach my desired goal of 215 pounds. Additionally, my body was far from the ultimate goal I had set for myself, which was to eventually have a six pack like few other 61-year-old men. After reaching 218 pounds, I hit a plateau and, regardless of my efforts in running, lifting, or dieting, I couldn't achieve the desired results. During the Christmas holidays that year, I kept receiving pop-up ads on my phone from my Livestrong app, which was advertising an eight-week physical challenge starting on January 11, 2016. I distinctly remember accepting the challenge on December 28th. Within just one month of starting High Intensity Interval Training (HIIT), I could already see the development of the six pack I wanted.

The training program I participated in consisted of six different workouts per week. All of the workouts were conducted via video and led by the renowned trainer Niki Holander. I'm sharing my fitness journey with you because I initially believed I had enough self-discipline and motivation to train on my own, without the assistance of a coach. However, I soon realized I was mistaken. I failed to engage in the one thing that Chief believes is challenging for most people: self-evaluation. Truthfully, I needed a coach and I needed to be open to coaching if I wanted to achieve my goals. Despite being a firm believer that everyone requires a mentor or coach, it was this experience that made me realize I needed to practice what I preach.

CHAPTER FOUR

Characteristic #4 – Self Discipline

Deep Practice

We've already determined that dribbling is one of the basic skills needed to play basketball effectively. If you try to play the game of basketball, particularly at the point guard position, without first mastering your dribbling skills, you will be destined to fail. Ironically, the game of life is no different when you see people trying to do something without proper preparation. It amazes me that people will go into an interview for their dream job without doing any research on the company or understanding what the job entails. In the game of basketball, we would say that this player didn't put together a scouting report.

The HR personnel that I have had an opportunity to talk to all seem to agree that the interviewees who get hired are typically those who arrive prepared for the interview. They also say that they can often recognize the interviewees who have the best opportunity to succeed in the job. They say they are able to predict their success because their interview preparation demonstrates that they were disciplined enough to do the preliminary work that would ensure they were adequately prepared to handle the interview successfully. If you think about this same scenario from a basketball perspective, it's clearly apparent that trying out for a basketball team and the interview process for a job are very similar situations. In each scenario, the players (people) had the discipline to be adequately prepared to make the team or land the job. Essentially, if you want to eventually live like no one else, you must be disciplined enough to live like no one else.

Let's face it, *discipline is discipline,* no matter what your walk in life. If you closely watch the practice (preparation) habits of the best basketball players, you'll recognize right away that they're never satisfied with their performance. Their lack of satisfaction is why they're willing to do what other players aren't willing to do, to perfect every aspect of their performance. To perfect their performance, they're willing to spend unimaginable hours working on their skill set, body, conditioning, and basketball IQ by watching film. Great players (people) understand three important keys that are related to success and require *self-discipline*, which unsuccessful players (people) lack: 1) *the distraction of premature satisfaction*, 2) *deep practice*, and 3) *discipline*. Of the three, the first one, *the distraction of premature satisfaction,* is the one that destroys success faster than the other two.

The best example of never giving in to the distraction of premature satisfaction that I can think of is (Chief) Tom Izzo. His sustained success as a coach can be directly related to the fact that he is never satisfied. He firmly believes that yesterday's success is nothing but old news, which is why he's constantly searching for new ways to improve himself as a coach. He's always on the phone with some of the best coaches in sports, including coaches outside the game of basketball. I remember watching how determined he was the day after we had just won the national championship, starting his pursuit of another championship right away. Here's what he did once we got back to East Lansing Tuesday afternoon following the championship game on Monday night. Every one of us, except Chief, was worn out from the night before. Of course, the celebration went well into the early morning hours of the next day. When we got back to East Lansing, Chief took our entire staff out to eat at a local Applebee's. After we finished eating, everyone was anxiously waiting to get home for some well-deserved rest, except for Chief, who had no interest in resting. He, on the other hand, was looking forward to driving three hours to Marion, Indiana, to watch Zach Randolph, formerly of the NBA's Memphis Grizzlies and Sacramento Kings. At the time, Zach was the best player in the country and our top recruit. That night, he was playing a game at his high school, and Chief made it a priority to go watch him play because he knew the impact it would make on Randolph if he showed up to watch him play the night after winning the National Championship game. Many coaches and people would have said to themselves, "I'm too tired and sleepy to drive three hours, especially after one of the biggest nights of their career." They would have just called the kid and gone to watch him play some other time. But that's not how Tom Izzo or any other self-disciplined person is wired.

Chief knew that the right time was now, no matter how inconvenient it might be to do what was right at that time. Tom knew that going now, rather than later, could help us acquire the kid and, in the big picture, increase the possibility of winning another National Championship the following season. As a result of what Tom did that night, we ended up acquiring Zach Randolph, and we came close to winning a second National Championship in 2001. However, we fell just one game short, losing to Arizona in the 2001 Final Four semifinal. Many people fail to understand that it is self-discipline, not motivation, that drives us to do the things we need to do when we really don't want to do them. Self-discipline must be a key part of your mindset if you desire to be great at whatever you want to do in life. Tom Izzo is a Hall of Famer because he never allows the distraction of premature satisfaction break his commitment to remaining disciplined and putting in the necessary hard work that is required to consistently achieve excellence. When I was a kid there was an old folks saying that went like this, "*satisfaction* for sure killed the cat (your dream)." At some point you have to *honestly self evaluate* ask yourself if *satisfaction* is killing your (cat) dream? This is a question that never gets honestly answered because most people have a hard time *honestly self evaluating themselves*.

The second key that successful people understand is the power of *deep practice*. The philosophy of *deep practice* is simply this: whatever you want to master, you must do it until it hurts. Chief

(Tom Izzo)'s continued success in the basketball world can be attributed to the philosophy of *deep practice*. If you ever have the opportunity to watch our team practice, you'll see the philosophy of *deep practice* at work. Chief believes that the only way you can achieve near-perfection is to practice until it hurts, which is an essential part of the *Deep Practice Philosophy*. He's a master at selling his team, his coaches, and even himself on the benefits of *deep practice*.

We often have other coaches observe our practices, and their post-practice comment is always the same: "Do you guys always practice that hard every day?" Secondly, they ask, "How do you have this kind of enthusiasm and energy every day in practice?" I tell them the answer is YES, and if you were here for every practice throughout the year, you would see that the effort, energy, and enthusiasm you saw on the first day of practice would be no different from what you would see on the last day of practice. It's part of our DNA to always practice until it *hurts* because it is *demanded*. The *Deep Practice Philosophy* is a significant part of what makes Tom Izzo a successful basketball coach. Similarly, success in the game of life is no different. Whatever your particular endeavor in life may be, if you want to achieve any degree of real success, you must first be willing to embrace the *Deep Practice Philosophy*.

The following is a great analogy, using the game of basketball to provide a clear explanation of what I am trying to say. Let's say you want to be a successful basketball player, but to achieve that, you must first master the fundamentals of the game from A to Z. To do that, you must develop the habit of deep practice. Similarly, if you want to be a successful businessman, you must relentlessly study every aspect of your business. To become an expert in each of those aspects, you must be willing to adhere to the philosophy of deep practice (study).

The *Deep Practice Philosophy* remains unchanged for individuals who push themselves to the limit, such as those who practice singing until their throat is in agony. Despite the pain, they persist in their practice because their desire to become a professional singer is so intense. Similarly, a piano player may practice until their hands are in excruciating pain, preventing them from continuing. An everyday example of the *Deep Practice Philosophy* is a father who works tirelessly day and night, sacrificing rest. Despite his exhaustion, he dedicates all his spare time, rather than sleeping on his days off work, to fully understanding the personalities, character, and thought processes of each of his children. He is fully aware that neglecting proper rest could eventually jeopardize his health or even his life. Yet, he doesn't care because being the best dad possible to his children means more to him than his own health. His thoughts may appear to be crazy, and I'm not advocating that you give up your health (*Remember Tom Brady*) to achieve your dreams. However, believe me, there are people who will risk their health, life, and limb to achieve the level of success they desire. Unfortunately, if you're not the kind of person who will at least work until it hurts, you'll have no chance to succeed if you're up against circumstances that threaten your success or if you're competing against someone who will work until it hurts.

The third key to success that successful people understand, which unsuccessful people don't grasp, is that discipline breaks the stronghold of the distraction of premature satisfaction. Moreover, they know that without self-discipline, you won't be able to maintain your commitment to deep practice. This commitment entails waking up early in the morning and working late into the night, putting in extra effort. It exemplifies the level of self-discipline required for success. In your effort to continually pursue success, fatigue, monotony, and self-doubt, if you're not self-disciplined, it will break your commitment to deep practice, and you'll give in to the distraction of premature satisfaction.

Again, let's use the game of basketball as an analogy to help you better understand the importance of self-discipline. In the game of basketball, to sustain the commitment needed to do the extra things that will make you an elite player, such as eating right, sleeping right, and spending extra time in film study, takes self-discipline. These are but a few of the extra things you'll need to commit to if you want to become an elite player. When frustration sets in because you're not getting immediate results from all the extra work, it will take self-discipline to push you through those negative thoughts and continue to stay focused on the task of being successful.

Throughout my entire career at Michigan State, I have never seen two kids more disciplined than Denzel Valentine and Bryn Forbes. As I previously mentioned, a typical day for them began with an early morning stretch or some sort of strength and conditioning training. This was usually followed up with some shooting or individual skill work. Then they were off to class, followed by study hall until our mid-afternoon team practice. On days when time permitted, they would come in before practice to watch thirty minutes of film. After practice, they'd shoot for another thirty minutes to an hour, depending on how well they shot the ball during practice that day. Next, it was twenty minutes in the cold tub and another thirty minutes getting stretched and receiving treatment for injury prevention. They would then shower, eat (the right foods), and come up to the office to watch more film. Before finally leaving to go home, they would take extra film with them of themselves or our next opponent to watch before they went to bed. This was their schedule day in and day out until the day they left Michigan State for professional careers in the NBA. Both Zel and Bryn never let the distraction of premature satisfaction keep them from reaching their ultimate goal of one day playing in the NBA, a goal they've both achieved because they simply remained self-disciplined.

CHAPTER FIVE

Characteristic #5 – The Gamer

"Be at your Best when your Best is needed"

Travis Trice

The outstanding play of Travis Trice, our little 5'10, 170-pound point guard, paved the way for our 2015 Final Four tournament run. Travis, although small in stature, was big in heart and the ultimate gamer. He was without question a high-performance, maximum Xecution player. Looking back, it was his extraordinary nine-game stretch that got us to the conference tournament championship game against Wisconsin and the Final Four semifinal championship game against Duke. During that run, Travis averaged 19 points and 5.7 assists per game. Those numbers earned him a spot on the Big10 All-Tournament team, and three weeks later, he was selected as the Most Outstanding Player of the NCAA East Regional.

However, that year, we struggled to win throughout the entire season. In fact, by late February, our team was in trouble with the possibility of missing the NCAA tournament because we had lost six of eight games in overtime. At the time, we didn't think that a record of 20-8 was good enough to get us into the tournament for the eighteenth consecutive season.

As a result, we headed into March without a quality win, with only three regular-season games left to play. We felt that if we couldn't win at least two of those last three games, our chances of making the tournament would be slim to none. In addition to the challenge of winning those games, we had to play two of them on the road against nationally-ranked teams.

Our first game was against Wisconsin on the road, who were at that time the second-ranked team in the nation and the first-place team in the Big10. Unfortunately, we ended up losing to them in a game we desperately needed to win for two reasons. First, we needed every additional win we could get to boost our overall record. Second, Wisconsin was a nationally-ranked team at the time, and a win over them would have given us a tremendous quality win for our tournament resume.

The loss to Wisconsin made our next game against Purdue a must-win game. Winning that game would not be easy, because the Purdue team was also nationally ranked and performing exceptionally well. Our team would have to play at a high-performance, maximum Xecution level to secure the victory. If the team didn't perform to the best of their abilities, we would need a player to step up and be at their best when their best is needed. Fortunately for us, that player was Travis Trice, one of the most courageous gamers I've ever been associated with throughout my entire coaching career. There is no doubt that without his 27-point performance, we would have lost to Purdue, and if that had happened, we would have lost any chance we had of making the NCAA tournament.

The only other chance we would have had left if we had lost would've been to win our conference tournament, a challenge that, in reality, would have been next to impossible. The reason is that we would have dropped below fourth place in the regular season conference standings. From that position, we would have been forced to play four games in the conference tournament to win it, as opposed to three games. This feat has only been accomplished once in Big Ten tournament history. However, we managed to win our last two regular season games and keep our hope of making the tournament alive.

Now, our next challenge would be to beat Ohio State, another nationally ranked team, that we barely defeated in our first game against them. They were led by DeAngelo Russell, their superstar player, who went on to become the second player taken in the 2016 NBA draft by the Los Angeles Lakers. It was no secret to our players and staff that the future of our season would be determined by the outcome of this game. We were fairly confident that if we could win the game, we would secure a spot in the NCAA tournament for the 18th straight season. The victory would provide our three seniors, Travis Trice, Branden Dawson, and Keenan Wetzel, not only an opportunity to compete in the tournament but also a chance to advance to the 2016 final four. An accomplishment realized by every four-year player throughout Tom Izzo's coaching career, with the only exceptions being the 2014 senior class of Adreian Payne and Keith Appling. However, as fate would have it, our 2015 senior class was able to realize their dream of playing in the 2015 Final Four because of Travis Trice's phenomenal *High Performance Maximum Execution* play throughout the entire tournament. His outstanding play solidified our spot in the tournament. In the game against Ohio State, he scored 18 points in a must-win Big Ten tournament game. He then turned around and scored 20 points the next day in our victory over Maryland in the conference tournament semi-final game. Although we lost to Wisconsin in the conference tournament championship game, it wasn't because Travis didn't show up to play, but rather due to his foul trouble throughout the entire game, an unforeseen factor completely out of his control. Looking back at our last nine games of the season, starting with Purdue and right up through our Elite Eight regional championship game against Louisville, there is a strong case that Travis's nine-game stretch of 19 points and 5.7 assists is one of the most extraordinary performances in Michigan State basketball history.

Gamers are gamers, whether it is in the game of life or the game of basketball. Confidence, focus, and determination are three common characteristics that separate gamers from all other players. Unlike most of us, these (people) players are a special breed. They're motivated by an internal belief driven by an astronomical level of confidence. They don't need external motivation from coaches or teammates to perform at their best.

The gamer always wants the game-winning shot, not because they're not afraid to take it, but because they know they will make it. You won't find doubt or fear in the gamer's DNA because they're just not wired that way. Contrary to popular belief, gamers aren't always born with the gift of extraordinary confidence. They are confident because they believe they have earned the right to be confident. Their level of confidence and ability to consistently execute at a high-performance maximum Xecution level is the result of their hard work, extra time, extra effort, and relentless hours of preparation dedicated to mastering their craft. Consequently, when it's time to perform at their best, confidence is never an issue for gamers. They believe that their preparation confirms their confidence. The key word here, regarding the gamer's confidence, is "belief." They understand that belief is the essential internal component needed to have the confidence required to be a gamer.

A lot of players put in the same amount of time, effort, and preparation as gamers, but they don't have the gamers' confidence because they don't believe they've earned that right. Throughout my coaching career, I've seen such players who aren't gamers for one simple reason: they lack belief. A lack of belief confirms the fact that they don't trust the readiness of their preparation. These same players, who are equally talented as most gamers and have everything it takes to be a gamer, yet they can't consistently perform at a high-performance maximum Xecution level because they lack confidence. As a result of their disbelief, they struggle when it comes time to step up and play at a high-performance maximum Xecution level. This happens because their disbelief and mistrust cripple their abilities to perform at their best under pressure.

Even though they possess the talent and ability to perform at their best when their best is needed, these individuals are the ones who should effortlessly make game-winning free throws with no time remaining on the clock, consistently making game winning

157

shots. However, due to their lack of confidence compared to a seasoned gamer, they are unable to consistently deliver their best when it is most needed. They seem to only excel in situations where they can dominate the game solely based on their raw talent, assuming that no opponent can match their level of talent. Nevertheless, when faced with equal talent and mounting pressure, they struggle to perform because they lack the confidence to truly believe in themselves and get the job done.

In the gamer's mind, the game is always the same game with just another name. In other words, the name of the game may change from basketball to auto sales, property development, business owner, father, husband, preacher, teacher, policeman, and the list could go on indefinitely depending on which occupation you choose to pursue in the game of life. No matter which occupation you choose, if you want to succeed, you'll have to be a gamer. To be a gamer, you will have to be the player (person) who, regardless of circumstances, is at his best when his best is needed. Because in the game of life, there are no level playing fields. Although most basketball players already know this, they seem to somehow forget it for some strange reason once they hang up the sneakers. In my mind, way too many guys don't seem to be able to translate the fact that a challenge is a challenge, whether it's on the basketball court or in the boardroom. Please BELIEVE me when I say that the pressure to make the game winning free-throws is no different than the pressure of closing a big business deal. Hitting the game winning shot takes the same mental toughness that it takes to land your dream job because you slam dunked the interview.

Our Michigan State 2019 Final Four, Big Ten, and Big Ten tournament championship team was a collection of gamers. The members of that team knew how to show up collectively, as gamers do, and be at their best when their best was needed. They were the most connected group in terms of playing together as a single-minded unit, more so than any other team we have ever coached. Their chemistry was amazing, which made them fascinating to watch. The only other team we had that matched their chemistry, of course, would be our 2000 national championship team.

The starting five of our 2019 team consisted of current NBA players Cassius Winston and Xavier Tillman, in addition to three high-level role players: Aaron Henry, Matt McQuaid, and Kenny Goins. Along with substitutes Nick Ward, Kyle Ahrens, Gabe Brown, and Marcus Bingham, all of them were willing to sacrifice their own individual talents to create a unique, selfless style of play that made them a championship team.

In every season, a team has a make-or-break turning point. That turning point for our 2019 team came as a result of a coaches' meeting with Tom, myself, and our three seniors: Cassius Winston, Matt McQuaid, and Kenny Goins, along with our junior center, Xavier Tillman. Coach called the meeting to discuss the possibility of Nick Ward returning to the starting lineup in place of Xavier Tillman. Xavier had replaced Nick in the starting lineup for seven games due to an injury to his hand.

The meeting began with Tom explaining to the guys why he believed it would be best to reinsert Nick into the starting lineup in order to maintain our team camaraderie and chemistry. However, the guys had different thoughts on the matter compared to Tom's. They all believed that removing Xavier from the starting lineup would be a big mistake and would ultimately disrupt our team chemistry. In fact, they understood better than Tom and myself how important it was for the lineup to remain intact for the ultimate success of our team. It wasn't that they felt Nick wasn't still a vital part of our team's success. They all expressed the fact that we needed Nick because he was an exceptional low-post scorer. However, during his time out with the injured wrist, the identity of our team shifted from relying solely on our offense to win, to becoming an exceptional defensive team as well. This shift occurred when X became the starter and played the majority of the minutes at the center position.

Gamers know how to dig deep and summon the determination to perform at their best, even when they are losing during the competition and emerge victorious in the game. In contrast, there are players who only excel when they are in the lead and never manage to come from behind to win. Our 2019 season serves as a prime example of why being a gamer leads to success, whether it's in basketball or in life. Throughout that season, we achieved several remarkable come-from-behind victories, which became a defining characteristic of our team. Our Elite 8 game against Duke was no exception, as we had to rally from behind to secure the win. Duke, at the time, was the top-ranked team in the nation, boasting a starting lineup comprised of four first-round draft picks and a talented bench player. As I mentioned earlier, we were a team of gamers, and it was Kenny Goins, our fifth offensive option, who ultimately sank the game-winning shot. I firmly believe that our ability to defeat Duke, against all odds, was solely due to one reason: we were a team of gamers.

Another commonly shared characteristic of *Gamers* is their ability to stay laser beam focus on the (task) game. The *Gamer'*s ability to center his total attention on the (task) game, both short and long term, gives him an enormous advantage over his opponents (competitors) that lack the ability to stay as focused as he does. The *Gamer* is able to direct his total concentration on the game (task) because he understands that to reach optimal peak performance, he must maintain his *focus*. This particular level of high concentration stimulates thought processes that are solely directed at executing what he must do to (succeed) win. The 2017 NBA championship series is a great example of what can happen when a team (company, family) loses its focus. Before losing their focus, the Golden State Warriors were up three games to one on the Cleveland Cavaliers then allowed them to come back and win the championship series, four games to three. "A feat accomplished only one other time throughout the entire history of the NBA, the Cavaliers were essentially beaten, down three games to one, before putting their total focus on playing their best, one possession at a time. This ultimately allowed them to achieve the impossible, winning three games in a row and, as a result, winning the NBA Championship."

To substantiate what happened, let's analyze the mindset of both teams. But before we do, let's talk about the single most dangerous enemy to maintaining focus: distractions. As a matter of fact, distractions can blindside even the best of us because they come at us in so many different ways. All too often, something you wouldn't think of as a distraction can manifest itself into one if you're not careful. Distractions don't always come in the form of something you would consider to be negative. For example, you might have the habit of staying up watching movies or playing video games all night. Research proves that anything less than eight hours of sleep has a negative effect on performance. That being said, even if you're the person who is always at home and never out drinking or partying all night, you're still not getting the necessary rest to be at your best when your best is needed.

After all, being up all night is the same whether you're at a club, watching movies, or playing video games. My point is this: there is no real difference between a person who stays up all night at home watching movies and playing video games, and a person who stays up all night drinking and socializing at a club. In both cases, you're not getting the necessary rest to perform at your best when you need to. The bottom line is that you've been blindsided by a behavior you never thought of as a distraction. Why? Because you're probably saying to yourself, "I'm at home... I'm not out at the nightclub like the other guys." But being at home doesn't mean you can let your guard down. You may be unaware that the video game you're playing can become a distraction if not properly managed. Before you know it, you've lost focus on the real reason you decided to stay home.

Once your focus shifts, you unknowingly find yourself blindsided by the distraction of playing video games. Without realizing it, you end up staying up all night. This happens to us because we tend to think of distractions as the result of bad behaviors, such as excessive drinking, smoking, or overeating, just to name a few. However, we rarely consider distractions as the result of poorly managed good behavior.

Let's use an analogy to illustrate what can happen if you're not careful. Imagine you're at home, but instead of utilizing your time to talk with your loved ones, family, and friends, you're always on the computer or your cell phone. Another example would be players who overtrain or people who are workaholics. They never get anything accomplished because they neglect to get proper rest. Hard work is commendable, but not at the expense of rest.

One distraction that some people are guilty of is overindulging in food and sex. Food becomes a distraction when it begins to jeopardize our appearance and the quality of our health due to overeating. In sports, there is a phrase commonly used amongst coaches and players alike. But for the sake of decency, I'll use the word "sex" rather than the P word normally used. The phrase goes like this: "Sex is undefeated." In other words, some players (people) get distracted and choose sex over staying focused on the task at hand. Believe me, I am well aware of the power of sex, but when a person (or player) becomes so distracted by it that it shifts their focus, it becomes a problem that hinders the pursuit of success. Good behaviors are only good when properly managed but can easily become distractions that can, once again, shift your focus.

Think about it: if you were to take inventory of your life, I would bet you'll find that it was a distraction that caused you to lose focus at some point and miss out on an opportunity you really wanted. As I mentioned previously, it was a distraction that caused the player (person) to shift the center of his attention from concentrating on his game performance (task) to staying up all night to satisfy his need for instant gratification. There is no doubt in my mind, especially in today's world, that the distraction of instant gratification has destroyed not only the immediate performance of a lot of players (people) but also their long-term goals and dreams. I've particularly seen this happen to young men under the age of twenty-five and, in some cases, immature older men. This happens because they want it all right now: the money, the women, the big house, expensive clothes, and cars.

Over the years, I've seen individuals who demonstrate this sort of behavior because they lack the necessary life experiences to deal with this form of distraction maturely. I've also witnessed this outrageous desire for instant gratification destroy the lives of many successful, full-grown men as well. These were men who were extremely successful at one point in their lives, men who were undoubtedly on their way to lifelong success and riches. I once witnessed this happen to a very successful restaurant entrepreneur. Shortly after he opened his first restaurant, he was blessed to open another, and then a third, downtown in a prime location. His businesses were doing well, but before he reached financial stability, the distraction of instant gratification put him out of business. Why? Because he started taking money away from his business to satisfy his need for instant gratification. Instead of reinvesting his money back into his business to facilitate continued growth, he ended up spending enormous amounts on indulgences such as good times, women, houses, and cars. The desire for instant gratification distracted him and led to the collapse of his gold mine, resulting in him losing everything he had built.

Let's use basketball as an analogy to explain this scenario in the context of a basketball player. His immediate goal could be to play at an all-star level in every game, while his long-term goal is to lead his team to a championship. Similarly, a young executive may aspire to make his division the top performer in the company as a short-term goal, positioning himself to one day become the CEO of the entire company as his long-term goal. In both cases, maintaining laser-like focus is crucial to achieving their goals.

Now let's go back to how all of this pertains to the 2017 NBA Championship series between the Golden State Warriors and the Cleveland Cavaliers. During that series, we saw the Warriors lose their focus because they became victims of the distraction of premature satisfaction. Up three games to one, they played the next three games without the same sense of urgency that had put them up three games to one in the series. As I previously mentioned, distractions can affect you in many different ways, and success can be one of them if not properly managed. This is exactly what happened to the Warriors after going up three games to one because they lost their sense of urgency. Why? Because they figured it would be impossible for the Cavaliers to beat them three games in a row, just as they had previously beaten the Cavaliers three games in a row. Although Draymond Green, Steph Curry, and Klay Thompson are elite gamers, they broke the cardinal rule commonly shared amongst all gamers.

The rule suggests that the gamer never allows himself to become a victim of his own success because a wise competitor knows the heart of other gamers. In this instance, that other gamer happened to be LeBron James, unarguably the best basketball player on the planet. At the beginning of this chapter, I mentioned that gamers are at their best when their best is needed. When the odds are stacked against him, a real gamer loves the challenge of being counted out because he uses it as extra motivation to play at the high-performance maximum Xecution level needed to (succeed) win. In fact, he embraces the challenge to (succeed) win in spite of having no one else in the world who believes he will win. By embracing the challenge, he ignites his innermost competitive spirit, which then triggers a burning desire to perform at a level that exceeds his normal performance. That is exactly what happened to LeBron James and his Cleveland Cavalier teammates.

His games 5, 6 and 7 performances were the greatest in NBA history by any individual player. The outcome of those performances resulted in a unbelievable, come-from-behind NBA Championship. Intelligent observers not only recognizes what can happen no matter what your particular endeavor, if you maintain total *focus* on the (job, goal) task at hand. The fact that this happened to three of the most *Elite Gamers* in the basketball world, is living proof that it can most certainly happen to anybody else. If you're going to achieve high level success in the *game of life, you'll have to be a Gamer.* Simply put, *get your game on*!!!

CHAPTER SIX

Characteristic #6 – Resilience "The Antidote for Adversity"

Playing Through Fatigue and Adversity

Tom Izzo

The best players in the game of basketball consider fatigue as an ally rather than an adversary. Therefore, they never give up because they understand that when adversity strikes, it is the first sign that their path to victory and success is inevitable. Adversity often comes with a level of fatigue that leads many players and people to quit. However, successful individuals perform at a high-performance maximum Xecution level despite the onset of fatigue. High performers can take pain and suffering and transform it into motivation that propels them through fatigue and the challenges associated with winning. All winners, whether in basketball or in life, clearly understand that to succeed at the highest level, they must consistently overcome adversity and fatigue. High performers know that they need to prepare both mentally and physically long before the day of their competition to be able to effectively perform when faced with adversity and the stronghold of fatigue.

Their training regimen must be so strenuous that it forces them to push themselves to the limits of their physical and mental capabilities. Their will to win (succeed) supersedes the pain and suffering that come with this form of training because they know it is the only way to develop the necessary mental strength, physical strength, and stamina needed to win (succeed) against their highest level of competition. The high performer knows that without a full commitment to this brutal training regimen, he won't be prepared to fight through the extremely high levels of fatigue and adversity brought on by the intensified level of competition that he will face. Consequently, he doesn't even question the process because he knows that those who do are forgotten about and never reap the rewards of (success) winning. The winners' (successful people's) mentality is to embrace the onset of fatigue and adversity because they instinctively know that their desired outcome is on the other side of the wall of resistance called fatigue and adversity. The 2016 NBA Championship series is a great analogy depicting the wall of resistance. Let's revisit what happened in the series with LeBron James and his Cleveland Cavalier teammates down 3 games to 1 against the Golden State Warriors in a best-of-seven games series. The Cavaliers, flat on their backs, were faced with the challenge of knocking down the wall of resistance called adversity. If they couldn't win the remaining three games of the series, their dream of winning the NBA championship would come to a dismal end. This would be a tall task that had only been accomplished by one other team in NBA history. However, the Cavaliers were prepared to meet this enormous wall of resistance they were facing because throughout the entire year, they had already faced similar walls of resistance throughout the season. As a result, they were prepared, willing, and able to break through the wall of resistance now facing them to claim the championship that they believed was rightfully theirs to win.

What most players (people) don't understand is that the same resistance they've faced as basketball players is no different than the resistance they will face in the game of life. The resistance blocking your success in the game of life will usually require you to deal with it mentally rather than physically. Because the mental strain associated with taking on adversity brings on a level of mental fatigue that will force most players (people) to give up and quit. Here is where a lot of players (people) fail because they're unwilling to fight through the mental fatigue that causes them to lose their will to fight through resistance. Tragically, I find this failed mentality to be a strange characteristic of some former basketball players. Because most of them grow up dealing with resistance every day while playing the game of basketball, it troubles me that many players can't make the analogy between the fatigue and adversity they experience on the court when an opposing defender (representing resistance) tries to prevent them from scoring. What they fail to realize is that the same resistance, adversity, and fatigue they face in basketball are the very challenges they will encounter in the game of life.

Once you decide to hang up your basketball shoes and step into the real world, please remember that anything worthwhile will require extraordinary preparation. As I mentioned previously, I don't understand why highly successful basketball players struggle to apply the same principles of preparation to their lives. These individuals may have been outstanding basketball players, but they often face difficulties in life because they fail to prepare themselves adequately to achieve their ambitions outside the game. Consequently, I have witnessed many of them miss out on great opportunities, such as dream jobs, simply because they were not adequately prepared for business meetings or interviews. It is interesting to note that these same individuals would never consider showing up to a basketball tryout (equivalent to an interview or business meeting) without first being properly prepared for it.

Tom Izzo left Northern Michigan University, where he was earning $26,000 a year as an assistant coach, to pursue his dream of becoming a Division I basketball coach. Little did he know the challenges he would face along the way. In hindsight, it turned out to be the right decision. Had he not left NMU to pursue his dreams in East Lansing, Michigan, he wouldn't be the person he is today. He started as a graduate assistant, earning $2,000 a year, working under Jud Heathcote at Michigan State. Jud had a reputation for being one of the toughest coaches to work for in college basketball. Let me make this clear: Coach Heathcote was a great guy, but when he put on his head coach's hat, he displayed a different side of himself that most people feared. This different side of Jud served as both a blessing and a curse in terms of what Izzo needed to learn about being a successful head coach. On several occasions, Izzo has shared with me that he was afraid of Jud every day, and that fear turned out to be a blessing. In fact, the methods Jud used to impart his lessons to Tom were tough and sometimes even brutal. I always tell young individuals who aspire to be like Tom Izzo that they need to be prepared to make significant sacrifices, such as giving up their left arm, right arm, both legs, some teeth, and enduring a lot of hardship for a considerable period of time.

Of course, most of them don't believe me because they all think that what Tom went through couldn't possibly have been that hard. Tom survived those hard times because he was smart enough to translate the lessons that he learned playing basketball to successfully break through the wall of resistance that forces people to give up on their dreams. His resolve to push through fatigue and adversity has earned him a spot in the National Basketball Hall of Fame as one of the all-time winningest coaches in the history of college basketball.

Throughout your entire life, you will experience the hardship of fatigue and adversity. During those times, fatigue will attack you physically, and at other times, mentally, and sometimes both. In a similar sense, adversity will present itself with both external and internal resistance. The life lesson from all of this is simple, uncomplicated, and easy to understand. Ultimately, you must be willing to fight through the wall of resistance and keep fighting until the resistance relents to your will to succeed.

CHAPTER SEVEN

Characteristic #7 – The Playmaker

"Can you make other (people) players better"

Draymond Green, Tom Izzo, Earvin (Magic) Johnson

The Chicago Bulls team of the 90s had both Michael Jordan and Scottie Pippen. Today, the Golden State Warriors have Steph Curry and Draymond Green. I specifically chose to recognize these two teams because they are the number one and number two all-time winningest teams in NBA history. These two teams are the epitome of *High Performance Maximum Xecution*. Although their eras of success are different, their struggles to consistently play at a championship level year after year are no different.

The Bulls held the record with 71 regular season wins until it was broken by the Golden State Warriors' 73 regular season wins in 2016. The unusual correlation between these two highly successful teams is that the playmakers on each team were two of their team's most talented players. In fact, all four were NBA All-Star caliber players. The value of the playmaker generally goes unappreciated by most fans and the media because their contributions can't be measured quantitatively in terms of numbers like scoring points, grabbing rebounds, or dishing out assists. A statistical sheet can't give you a clear picture of the total impact of their contributions in terms of winning a game. Because it doesn't always indicate which player's performance really determined the outcome of the game, especially from a defensive perspective.

In essence, as I previously stated, a playmaker's value to his team cannot be measured by the number of points he had, but rather his contributions have to be measured by things in the game that are, for the most part, immeasurable. Most fans and media people don't always appreciate the fact that playmakers can win games for their team without scoring a single point.

Draymond Green of the Golden State Warriors demonstrated exactly what I'm talking about when he became the first player in the history of the NBA to record a triple-double without scoring in double figures. In that game, he only scored 4 points, but he had 12 rebounds, 10 assists, and 10 steals. These numbers suggest that even though he only scored 4 points, he completely dominated the game. His contributions throughout the game in terms of assists, rebounds, and steals made his teammates much better players in that game. His 12 rebounds specifically gave his teammates the opportunity to score easy baskets because they felt free to run the floor without worrying about staying back to help rebound. His 10 assists allowed his teammates to make easy, uncontested shots. Last but not least, the most impressive thing in my mind was his 10 steals, which forced the opponent into 10 turnovers, accounting for 40 of his team's points. Let me explain why: in theory, each turnover a team has counts as 4 points—the 2 points the opponent didn't score and the 2 points your team gets as a result of the turnover. Essentially, Draymond created ten four-point scoring opportunities that added additional value to each of his teammates' baskets scored from his steals.

To properly evaluate the performance of the *playmaker*, you must also include the effect his *intangible winning traits* have on his team's *success. The seven intangible winning traits* are significant factors that affect *winning*, which a statistic sheet can't account for, such as *leadership, playing energy, and intelligence. Intangible winning traits* cannot be *measured* in terms of the *positive influence* they have on a team's *overall performance. the seven intangible winning traits* play an enormously significant role in how hard a team plays and the team's ability to *effectively execute game-winning strategy.* All *winning (successful) teams (organizations)* have *talent*, but there is no one more *valuable* to a *winning (successful) team (organization)* than its *playmaker,* whose only ambition is to *win games and make his teammates better players.* The *unappreciated value* of the *playmakers'* selfless play is *immeasurable* and normally *goes unrecognized* because most people don't understand that *talent can't win without a playmaker to orchestrate its performance.* How many times have you seen *super talented teams* that can't (succeed) *win games* because they don't have a *playmaker* to manage the seven *intangible winning traits needed to consistently bring about the high-performance maximum Xecution needed to win games, as part of the team's culture*?

The value of the playmaker is just as important in the game of life as he or she is in the game of basketball. If your ambition is to be a highly successful individual, organization, or even a family, you will have to become a playmaker if you're not already. If you're not comfortable in the role of playmaker, don't let your ego stand in the way of finding someone who can be a playmaker for you. Most people are playmakers to some degree without ever realizing it because they very rarely recognize when they've made a positive impact on another person's life. This lack of self-analysis regarding people seeing themselves as playmakers is why I don't think the role of playmaker is respected. Therefore, a lot of people subconsciously serve as playmakers without even realizing that's what they're actually doing. I'll use myself as an example. Looking back, I never really saw myself as a teacher/coach. It was Tom Izzo and Mr. James Richendollar who saw the teacher/coach in me. When they did, both of them set out to literally force me into the teaching/coaching profession. Had neither man decided not to take on the role of playmaker to help me understand what was glaringly apparent to them, what my life's ambition should be, I would have never realized what I believe to be my God-given calling. From the cradle to the grave, we continually encounter people who serve as playmakers to us, as well as us to other people.

Now that I've matured into my manhood, I find myself often reflecting on all the different individuals who played significant roles in my life, shaping me into the man I've become today. One such person is Mr. James Richendollar, who eventually became the best superintendent in the history of the Van Buren Public School System in Belleville, Michigan. He taught me how to see meaningful relationships in people and how to utilize that knowledge to help them become better individuals.

Another important figure in my life is my cousin Calvin Dishmon, who taught me the value of considering different perspectives before making decisions. He emphasized the importance of looking at things from various angles.

My mother, Verda Claybrooks-Clark, taught me that love endures the test of time, even in the worst situations. Despite challenging circumstances, she showed me the power of love and its ability to persevere.

Additionally, Miss Mattie Grant taught me the true meaning of the African proverb, "Two people can have a child, but it takes a village to raise that child." She has dedicated her life to being a mother figure to other people's children in our hometown, which also happens to be her own village. She invested as much time in raising me as she did in raising her own three sons.

It was my cousin James Seed, the toughest little man, inch for inch, pound for pound, I've ever seen in my entire life. He taught me that "It's not the size of the dog in the fight, but more importantly, it's about the size of the fight in the dog." Keith Simons, my best friend, taught me to never allow bitterness to break your spirit. His willingness to remain positive despite going through a heart-wrenching divorce that left him both homeless and heartbroken, and later battling cancer that tragically ended his life prematurely. Yet, through it all, he never complained or felt sorry for himself. As a matter of fact, he felt even more obligated to get to work every day, in spite of being sick from chemo treatments. He did it because he felt it was his job, come hell or high water, to be there for the people he worked with every day. Then there was Lolakate Williams, a childhood friend from whom I learned to overcome challenges. At the time, I was too young to realize all the amazing things she could do despite her handicap. When she was 11 or 12 years old, she was caught in a house fire that nearly took her life. By the grace of God, she survived, but not without damage to her brain. She was left crippled on one side of her body and paralyzed on the other. Nevertheless, through therapy and with the help of her loving grandparents, Mr. and Mrs. Williams, she was able to learn to walk and regain partial use of her left hand. Despite having only partial use of her hand, she possessed an amazing talent for art. Her drawings and paintings showcased some of the most spectacular pictures you could ever see. However, her artistic abilities were not the only thing that made her special; she also had a gift for teaching.

Before I was old enough to go to school, her grandmother would ask my grandmother if my three sisters and I could come to their house and play with Kate. Without hesitation, my grandmother agreed. In fact, every morning, she would get us dressed, feed us, and then send us to Kate's house to play. Despite her slight brain damage, Kate made sure to teach us everything she knew. My sisters and I learned how to tie our shoes, recognize colors, count, recite our ABC's, learn some sight words, and even how to draw and paint, all thanks to Kate. Despite her brain injury, Kate made it a point to teach us everything she knew, and she did so with great care and dedication.

As I write this, tears stream down my face as I think about Kate, because to this day, I believe I unknowingly broke her heart. As I grew older and developed an interest in sports, I didn't spend as much time with Kate as I used to. I still vividly remember running past her house every day to get to my backyard ball games, while she waited on the porch for me to stop and spend some time with her. But now, regretfully, I would just wave and yell hi as I selfishly ran up the street, never taking the time to think about how bad she must have felt. Although I was very young at the time, I was still old enough to see the hurt in her eyes as I ran past her every day. Unfortunately, a few years later, Kate died from complications of pneumonia. She was just 24 years old. Looking back, I now know that she was the ultimate playmaker in my life. She always put the happiness of others in front of her own. Often, I think God kept her here just for myself and my sisters. Than when He felt that she had completed her work with us, He decided to take her to be with Him. Because stupid people like myself no longer deserved her immeasurable loving kindness.

The Lord knew she had more than earned her heavenly rewards, and to receive her just rewards she had to depart from this world and ascend into the kingdom of heaven. To this day, I believe she is one of my guardian angels. I can't prove it, but I know it deep within my heart. In fact, what I do know for sure is that she was my most influential playmaker. Today, I am living proof of what I know for sure. There are still others I have to mention, like Dwayne Jones, one of my college teammates, who taught me that you must confront certain realities in life. I saw him walk his talk when he tragically lost his son. My grandfather, Dave Seed, was another one of my playmakers who taught me to always have confidence in myself as a young boy. He made me believe I could do anything, but he also emphasized the importance of having the confidence to do anything.

Then another one of my playmakers was William Eddie, my college teammate. He constantly reminded me of what my grandfather had taught me, even though he wasn't aware that he was doing it. And he's still doing it today. For that reason, I love him and owe him more than he will ever know.

Zach Hicks, another college teammate of mine, has taught me the power of unconditional friendship and love over the years. I am forever indebted to him for that. And then there's Leon Birdyshaw, who taught me the value of sacrifice. He sacrificed his own dream of being the head basketball coach at Belleville High School and turned the job over to me because he believed it would change the direction of my life. Obviously, he was right, and for that, all I can say is that I love you, man. Every one of these great individuals are playmakers who, at different times throughout my life, unknowingly helped me achieve things that I never dreamed possible.

The success I've had throughout my career ultimately goes back to their selfless contributions of time, effort, and energy spent mentoring, educating, and pushing me to fulfill my destiny. Yet there are so many more that I didn't mention because it would take this entire book to list every one of them. Respectfully, I would be remiss if I didn't add a few more to my list of *Special Playmakers*: Lloyd Carr, Mr. Emerson, Denny Easley, Mike Jones, Uncle Lamar and Aunt Rose, Wesley Charles, Johnny Reed, Mark Montgomery, Dwayne Stephens, Brian Gregory, and Doug Herner, Stan Heath, Tom Crean, and all the guys that I coached in both high school and college. I wish that I could name every one of you, but I think you all understand that it would be impossible for me to do so because there are so many of you who hold a special place in my heart. To each of you, I want to say thanks for all the plays you made so that I could be more than just a winner (successful), but ultimately become a champion in this game called life.

Let me emphasize this point: no matter your life's ambition, there will come a time when you must step into the role of a playmaker. Whether you're launching your own business, rising to the top as a CEO, or shaping the lives of your children as a parent, you'll inevitably find yourself in this role. To be an effective playmaker, you must embody these three key traits from my previously discussed '7 Intangible Winning Traits': Leadership, Energy, and Intelligence.

These three traits have a profound, yet hard-to-quantify, impact on achievement, performance, and execution. From my own experience, I know they are consistently present in all forms of success - personal, team-based, or organizational. Let's begin with Leadership. A leader's duty is to ensure that the goals and aspirations of any individual, team, or organization they're working with are well-defined and understood.

These three winning traits, all stemming from effective leadership, are as follows: 1) Performance: The overall performance of an individual, team, or organization is a direct result of effective leadership.2) Energy: The intensity or effort (how hard they work) an individual, team, or organization puts into their tasks is determined by their energy.3) Intelligence: The ability to successfully carry out a strategy hinges on the intelligence of your players (or people).

The role of an effective leader is to inspire their team, organization, or individuals they work with to consistently perform at a high level. The best way to achieve this is by encouraging everyone to contribute to the overall success of the team, organization, or individual. The outdated notion of "It's amazing what can be accomplished when nobody cares who gets the credit" no longer applies in today's world of social media and self-promotion. However, effective leaders understand the importance of being egoless and can motivate their team members to invest in the group's success. They actively listen to the ideas and suggestions of every member, whether they are part of a team, organization, or an individual they are responsible for. When wearing the hat of the playmaker the effective leader must discern how best to motivate each individual within a team or organization. Their aim is to inspire everyone to work at their maximum level of performance and Xecution, for the benefit of all.

An effective leader understands that everyone in an organization, whether they are a CEO or a custodian, wants to feel that their contributions are meaningful. The best leaders ensure that every team member, every individual they work with, feels that their work is integral to the success of the team or organization.

Great leaders, often likened to playmakers in a team sport, excel in using their leadership skills to manage their people effectively. One crucial trait that contributes to a leader's success is their work energy, which can be likened to a player's energy in a game of basketball. This energy is often the best tool a leader has to gain the trust of their team. When team members see that a leader is genuinely energetic and dedicated, they understand that the leader is authentic and committed to the success of the team, the organization, or the individual.

A high level of energy in a leader acts as a motivator, driving team members to work enthusiastically and perform at their highest levels to meet their goals. However, a leader is also aware that hard work alone won't lead to success. If the team members lack the necessary enthusiasm and energy to outperform their competitors, they won't be able to compete effectively and achieve their goals.

The energy and enthusiasm displayed by leaders can become infectious, spreading throughout an entire team, organization, or even impacting the individual they're coaching. When this happens, the mindset of the group or individual shifts to one of achievement and possibility. In 1998, the year of our first NCAA tournament appearance, we lost in the Sweet 16 game to North Carolina, who were the No.1 team in the country at the time. Immediately following the loss, Chief (Tom Izzo) called a team meeting in the hotel ballroom. No one, including myself or our staff, knew what he was about to discuss. That night, he spoke to us with a level of conviction, energy, and enthusiasm that resonated with every coach and player in the room. By the time he finished, every team member was committed to reaching the Final Four the following season.

From that moment, the commitment to reach the 1999 Final Four the next year was infused with an incredible sense of urgency among every player and coach in the program. It's unquestionable in my mind that Chief's (Tom Izzo) passionate speech that night set us all on a path to strive for the Final Four the next season. He convinced every player and coach that we could make our dream a reality if we focused solely on achieving that goal. The following season, no other team in the country could match our energy. As a result, we dominated the Big 10 with a 15-1 record as regular season conference champions, then won the Big10 Tournament Championship. Our winning streak continued until we lost to Duke in the Final Four.

In the book of Genesis, there's a story of men deciding to build a tower reaching to heaven. God realized that they might succeed if he didn't intervene, so he confounded their languages to prevent them from completing the tower. This story is known today as the Tower of Babel.

The two previous anecdotes demonstrate that energy isn't merely physical, but rather is the embodiment of one's internal willpower to manifest what you desire into physical existence. According to the Bible, the power of life and death lies in the tongue, suggesting that what you desire in life, you must first speak into existence. That night in the hotel ballroom, Chief did exactly that. Whether he intended to or not, I can't say for sure. What I do know is that Tom Izzo rarely does anything unintentionally. Sometimes, we become so consumed with a dream that our spirit compels us to bring it to fruition by speaking it into existence, even if we're not consciously aware of this process.

As a high school coach, I always began my pre-game talks with three essential phrases: "Play *hard*," "Play *smart*," and "Play *together*." These three principles are interconnected with the three *intangible winning traits* I mentioned before: *leadership, playing energy*, and *intelligence*. Each trait is crucial for the *Playmaker* to effectively lead the players. In my opinion, the most important phrase is "Playing *smart*," which emphasizes the use of intelligence. Successful teams, organizations, and individuals always have a *game-winning strategy, business plan*, or *method* to achieve their goals. To execute such plans and strategies, your *team* or *organization* needs individuals who are intelligent. I believe that, in most cases, these individuals are your *Playmaker*. If your *team* or *organization* is fortunate enough to have multiple *Playmaker*, you gain a significant advantage over your competition.

To lead effectively, the playmaker understands the importance of devising an intelligent plan of action. In the game of basketball, a successful playmaker possesses a deep understanding of the game plan, surpassing even their teammates. They are well-versed in their team's strengths and weaknesses, as well as those of their opponents. Furthermore, they have a keen awareness of their teammates' playing characteristics and roles, recognizing the significance of each role in the team's overall success.

Applying this concept to the game of life, being an effective playmaker necessitates being the most informed individual within your team or organization. In contrast to basketball, the plays you make in the game of life are of greater consequence, but the fundamental principles remain the same. Therefore, strategic and intelligent planning must take precedence in your pursuit of success in life.

A prime example of successfully transferring playmaking skills from basketball to life can be found in Earvin "Magic" Johnson's accomplishments in the business world. After retiring from professional basketball as one of the greatest players of all time, he used his exceptional playmaking skills to establish a highly successful multi-billion-dollar company. He currently holds the positions of owner/president at Earvin Magic Johnson Enterprises and is a significant shareholder in the Los Angeles Dodgers. I once had the opportunity to ask him a question that profoundly changed my perspective on success in the business world. I asked, "Earvin, how did you become proficient in making million-dollar business deals without any prior experience or background in business?" He replied, "Coach, it's simple. If 2+2 doesn't equal 4, there's no deal." Essentially, he meant that if someone couldn't explain a deal to him in a way that he could understand, they wouldn't reach an agreement. He reiterated that if someone presented him with a contract where 2+2 didn't add up to 4, there would be no deal. It's that simple Coach.

I previously mentioned that you need intelligence to be an effective playmaker. However, in this case, contrary to my belief, the greatest playmaker in basketball or possibly in life taught me in a brief conversation that understanding the genius of simplicity is more important than being the most intelligent person. He showed me that you don't have to be the most intelligent player to be the most successful playmaker. What I mean by the genius of simplicity is that you must be intelligent enough to recognize that 2+2 must equal 4. In summary, regardless of who you are or what your life dreams and ambitions may be, they will remain mere dreams and ambitions unless you can make impactful and life-altering moves and decisions. Successful individuals, or "players," understand the importance of being a playmaker in order to achieve success in the game of life. Being a playmaker doesn't require any special talents; anyone can do it, especially if your primary goals are to succeed and uplift those around you to the same level of success. It doesn't matter your size, race, religion, or background. Ultimately, your ability to be a playmaker is solely within your control. Interestingly, some of the greatest playmakers in both basketball and life come from small towns, such as Tom Izzo from Iron Mountain, Michigan, Draymond Green from Saginaw, Michigan, and Earvin (Magic) Johnson from Lansing, Michigan. They are ordinary individuals who have achieved extraordinary things in the game of life. The choice is yours. Choose to be a playmaker!

BONUS CHAPTERS

GREAT PLAYERS HAVE A GREAT FIRST STEP

Alan Anderson

The first step is crucial in every journey, whether it's on the basketball court or in life. In the game of basketball, a strong first step is a player's most powerful weapon on offense. It allows them to quickly go by their defender and become unstoppable. However, in today's basketball, it's rare to find players who possess a great first step.

There are two main reasons why players today often lack a great first step in basketball. Firstly, many players don't give enough respect to the skill and therefore don't invest the necessary effort to learn it. Secondly, the overall understanding of the basic fundamentals required for a great first step is lacking among a significant number of players today.

This deficiency in sound fundamentals can be attributed to the exceptional athleticism seen in today's players. Unfortunately, this heightened athleticism has resulted in an overreliance on speed and quickness, overshadowing the development of essential skills such as a highly effective first step. Throughout the history of the game, star players of the past relied heavily on a great first step as a go-to move. However, due to the athleticism prevalent in today's players, coaches and trainers often overlook the importance of emphasizing this skill in modern basketball.

When examining the essential skills needed for an effective and powerful first step, it becomes clear that successfully maneuvering around a defender relies more on executing the basic fundamental components of the first step rather than relying solely on speed and quickness. These fundamental components consist of three key elements: 1) stride length, 2) the player's ability to push the dribble ahead of themselves, and 3) positioning their shoulders below the defender's shoulders. It is worth noting that many respected commentators, analysts, and broadcasters often describe a player's first step as quick when discussing it on radio or television. However, in the case of a non-athletic player who is consistently going by their defender, they might label him as slow overall but has a quick first step.

The description of the *first step* provided is misleading and confusing for listeners, especially young and inexperienced players. It does not accurately explain the fundamental components of the skill. The commentators mistakenly describe the *first step* in a way to quickly explain to listeners how a player uses it to go around their defender, but they are not intentionally trying to mislead the audience. However due to time constraints, they are unable to provide a thorough explanation of the technique required to execute a *great first step properly.*

Alan Anderson, a standout player for the Spartans, possessed exceptional mastery of the *first step*. His proficiency stemmed from dedicated development of its three fundamental components. Alan belongs to a select group of elite players across all levels of basketball, past and present, who possess a *first step* that few can replicate. Undoubtedly, he is one of the most underrated players to have worn the Spartan uniform. In fact, his remarkable four-year career with the Spartans culminated in four consecutive outstanding performances during the 2005 tournament, leading the team to the final four. It may surprise many Spartan fans to learn that Alan also enjoyed a 13-year professional career, including seven years in the NBA. These accomplishments serve as undeniable evidence of his exceptional talents and the underrated nature of his career.

Upon reflecting on the conclusion of this book, I couldn't help but think of Alan and a quote from Stephen Covey's well-known book, "First Things First." Covey advises us to always start with the end in mind. This means that regardless of the path we're on in life, it's essential to envision our desired outcome before taking the first step. When we have a clear destination in mind, we can then create a well-thought-out plan to navigate the journey and reach our ultimate goal.

Covey's thoughts on how to start your journey have influenced my own perspective on how to end it. While I agree with Covey to some extent, I believe that you should "Always finish with the beginning in mind." In other words, as you approach the end of your journey, it's important to reflect on the beginning and not lose sight of the fundamental principles that enabled you to take the first step.

Many people reach the end of their journey but struggle to cross the finish line because they have lost sight of what got them started in the first place. This is where the concept of "finishing with the beginning in mind" becomes crucial. Alan Anderson, a successful basketball player, fully grasped the importance of this idea. He understood that his exceptional first step on the court would be meaningless if he couldn't follow through and finish with a made basket.

Alan recognized that he needed to invest the same amount of time, hard work, and diligence in developing his ability to finish plays as he did in perfecting his first step. Without the skill to finish effectively, his great first step would have been worthless. His way of thinking can be equally applied to both the game of basketball and life. Alan realized early on in his career that without an effective first step, it would be very difficult for him to consistently position himself to (succeed) score. He has also implemented this same philosophy to successfully run multiple businesses now that he has retired from the game.

The following three basic fundamental components of the first step in the game of basketball also translate into having a great first step in the game of life. These three basic fundamental components of the first step in the game of basketball can be meaningful concepts in terms of success when properly translated into what it takes to have a great first step in the game of life.

The first of these three components is the understanding and development of stride length. This technique is used to cover as much distance as possible in one step. In the game of basketball, stride length, when properly executed, gives you an immediate advantage over the defender guarding you, which usually results in an opportunity to score.

The concept of *stride length* can be applied to the game of life in a meaningful way. Once you have determined your life's journey, the preparation you undertake before taking the *first step* is comparable to the *stride length* in basketball. My coaching career serves as a prime example of this concept. When I made the decision to become a basketball coach, I recognized the importance of honestly evaluating myself first. Consequently, I discovered that despite my extensive experience as a lifelong player, I was far from ready to effectively coach a team. This realization prompted me to become a dedicated student of the game from a coach's perspective. It became apparent just how much I still had to learn. This awakening taught me that to succeed as a basketball coach, I needed to focus on mastering the fundamental aspects of team play. When you examine successful individuals in the game of life, you'll find that they are unafraid to ask themselves tough questions, identifying their shortcomings and weaknesses that hinder their success.

The second fundamental component of the first step in the game of basketball is the ability to push the dribble ahead of you, which helps you increase your stride length. This is important because having the dribble ahead of you allows you to cover more ground, making it easier to reach the basket and score. This analogy can be applied to life, where keeping your dreams ahead of you gives you a head start and a better chance of success compared to your competition. By staying focused on your goals and dreams, you can beat others to the finish line and achieve what you desire. For example, let's say you've started a business and you need a significant contract to take your startup to the next level.

Wisely you want to keep your dribble ahead of you as you use a friend who has a relationship with the CEO of the company you are negotiating with in order to leverage the deal. The third and final component of an effective and first step is to maintain a stride length that allows you to keep your shoulders below the defender's shoulders. This will help you gain and maintain leverage and momentum over the competition, preventing the defender from recovering and repositioning themselves to prevent you from (succeeding) score. This same fundamental component of the first step, keeping your shoulders below the defender's shoulders, is also a meaningful concept in the game of life. It relates to being (successful) scoring in various aspects of life. The ability to sustain and maintain your position in life is crucial for continuously gaining and maintaining the necessary leverage and momentum to overcome any opposition or defense that tries to hinder your success.

In the game of life, the opposition (defender) can come in various forms. Here's an example that demonstrates how to gain and sustain leverage and momentum. Imagine your objective is to secure a significant contract. To achieve this, you make the strategic decision to restructure your company's production methods. This allows you to meet your client's requirements efficiently while ensuring cost-effectiveness and maintaining profitability for your company. By staying ahead of competitors vying for the same contract, you increase your chances of success.

I believe that the basic fundamentals that contribute to having a great first step in the game of basketball also apply to having a great first step in the game of life. This will help you achieve your desired success. Once you have finished reading this book, I encourage you to search for Mat Ishbia on Google. He is one of our former players, whom I mentioned earlier, and he used the same fundamental characteristics discussed in this book to build a successful Fortune 500 company. Believe me, you can be just as successful as Mat if you are willing to master the basic fundamental components associated with having an effective first step.

In summary, it is essential to maintain a holistic perspective throughout your journey. Remembering the beginning and staying focused on the fundamentals will ensure that your efforts lead to a successful conclusion.

PLAYING GREAT DEFENSE GUARDS AGAINST UPSETS
Gary Harris

In the game of basketball, there is a commonly used phrase that emphasizes the importance of defense in winning championships. While scoring points is crucial, it becomes evident in every game throughout a season that the winning team must also excel in defensive play. Although there are occasional exceptions, such as when one team is exceptionally accurate with their shots while the other struggles, the majority of successful teams, especially at the highest level of play, reach a point where great defense is necessary for victory. Players on winning teams understand that to secure championships, they must excel as a team defensively.

When two teams with equal talent are evenly matched, it is inevitable that one team will eventually gain a lead over the other. At this point, the team with the lead must focus on protecting it by playing great defense. Contrary to popular belief, being elite in basketball is not solely determined by offensive skills. In fact, there are many elite players who have earned their status through
188

their exceptional defensive abilities. These elite defensive players are highly valued by their teams because they excel at safeguarding end-of-game leads with their game-winning defensive plays. Gary Harris is one such elite defensive player who initially played for the Denver Nuggets and now is a member of the Orlando Magic in the NBA.

During his time at Michigan State, he had an outstanding two-year college career. In his sophomore year, he stood out as both the best scorer and defender on our team, as well as in the Big Ten and arguably in all of college basketball. His exceptional defensive skills caught the attention of NBA scouts, and he was eventually selected in the first round of the draft by the Denver Nuggets. The Nuggets were so impressed by his defensive prowess that they offered him a lucrative contract worth eighty-five million dollars.

If you closely examine Gary's career, you'll notice that his commitment to great defense extends beyond the basketball court. From his early days playing 10 and under AAU basketball up to his professional career, he consistently played alongside and against players who were nearly two years older than him. Despite being one of the youngest players on his teams, he displayed remarkable maturity. He always prioritized protecting his career path, which translated into his strong defensive play on the basketball court—defending leads and securing victories.

Overall, Gary's dedication to defensive excellence has become a defining aspect of his playing style and a mindset he carries in all aspects of his life.

He has always been conscientious about defending and protecting his image, integrity, and character because he knows that a damaged reputation could hinder his opportunities in basketball or other endeavors. This is why successful individuals in the game of life also prioritize safeguarding their reputation.

They understand that a single mistake can tarnish their image and have detrimental financial and career consequences. They make it a habit to avoid behaviors that could jeopardize their chances of success, similar to how turnovers in basketball can change the outcome of a game. Turnovers are unforced mistakes resulting from careless or reckless decisions. In basketball, upsets often occur due to these senseless turnovers.

For readers unfamiliar with the term, as it relates to the game of basketball. An upset occurs when a strong team loses to a weaker team. As previously mentioned, this often happens due to turnovers resulting from poor decisions. When upsets happen in life, they are similar to those in basketball—caused by bad decisions. It is undeniable that bad decisions have led to the downfall of many individuals who were on the path to success, as they wasted their opportunities due to turnovers in the game of life. There is a long list of turnovers associated with failure in life, including drug and alcohol abuse, domestic violence, and extramarital affairs. Additionally, poor physical and mental health, unhealthy diet, lack of exercise, and ineffective stress management contribute to these failures. To avoid these detrimental mistakes, one must be willing to protect oneself by playing great defense against them.

It is essential that you take responsibility for devising a well-thought-out plan to manage your career path wisely. This plan should safeguard you against making costly mistakes that could potentially result in the loss of everything you have worked hard for or are currently striving to achieve. Before crafting your plan, take the time to thoroughly evaluate yourself and identify any pitfalls in your lifestyle that may lead to such detrimental mistakes. Once you have done that, it's crucial to develop a proactive strategy that shields you from falling into those pitfalls both now and in the future.

Naturally, a key component of your plan should focus on managing your finances effectively and avoiding risky situations such as substance abuse, domestic violence, extramarital affairs, and behaviors that promote poor health habits. These are just a few examples of the numerous pitfalls that could have severe consequences if not properly addressed. Remember, the best way to avoid a (setback) upset in the game of basketball or life is to play great defense.

CHIEF

Tom Izzo

Many people assume that Chief, being born in the U.P., embodies the typical Upper Peninsula outdoorsman who enjoys hunting, fishing, camping, and other wilderness activities like ice fishing, four-wheeling, and snowmobiling that interest most residents of the area. However, this assumption is incorrect as he doesn't have any fondness for these outdoorsman activities commonly enjoyed by those raised in the Upper Peninsula of Michigan. It's important not to portray Tom as someone who doesn't want to have fun or dislikes the outdoors altogether, because he does engage in outdoor activities that he genuinely enjoys. Golfing is one such activity, and he happens to be very skilled at it. In fact, he once beat a professional golfer during a celebrity practice round. Additionally, he finds great pleasure in spending time on the water, indulging in activities like boating and jet skiing. During his teenage years, Tom was actually quite proficient as a trick water skier.

One of Tom's most unpleasant experiences as a young head coach occurred because he disliked rugged outdoor activities. In the early years of his career, the university president at the time, Peter McPherson, asked him to participate in a week-long alumni event held at a dude ranch in Wyoming.

I can't help but laugh every time I think about it because he would call me every day, venting about how much he despised being there. He simply had no interest in riding horses and lassoing cows.

Tom, like anyone else, cherishes leisure time, fun, and quality moments with family and friends. He prefers not to isolate himself from others. Instead, he much rather enjoys hosting gatherings that typically involve family, friends, co-workers, and sometimes even casual acquaintances and strangers. His exceptional ability to make people feel at ease around him is unparalleled to anyone I have ever known. I often come across people who unexpectedly met Tom and couldn't believe that he took the time to stop and engage in a conversation with them. Additionally, Tom is known for his outgoing personality and quick wit. He has a deep love for comedy, with the late great Redd Foxx being his favorite comedian.

During our journey to the Final Four tournament in 1999, we found a great way to relieve stress during our downtime at the hotel: watching "The Kings of Comedy" video tape. It became a favorite pastime for our players and coaching staff, but no one enjoyed it more than (Chief) Tom Izzo. His laughter was the loudest and most contagious.

Tom thrives on challenges. If you want to witness his true potential, just present him with a difficult task. He is determined to overcome obstacles and achieve outstanding results. This side of him was evident on August 27th, 2022, when I experienced a life-threatening incident of ventricular fibrillation. From my immediate family to the doctors, nurses, and hospital staff, everyone witnessed Tom's incredible commitment to ensuring I received the best possible care. He went above and beyond, doing whatever it took to make sure I was getting the best of care.

192

Yes, it's true that he is not afraid of confrontation, but he knows how to effectively communicate his point and achieve his goals. Whether it involves finding a common ground or engaging in constructive discussions, he is skilled at getting his message across. He enjoys problem-solving, but he dislikes reactive situations that arise because someone, including himself, failed to anticipate and address the problem earlier. These situations could have been prevented if a proactive approach had been taken.

Working for him can be challenging because he is determined to succeed and expects results from his players and coaches. However, he holds himself to the same standards and doesn't ask anything of them that he wouldn't do or hasn't already done himself.

Chief's all-time superhero is Muhammad Ali, and his first opportunity to meet Ali was a complete coincidence. Neither Chief nor Ali had arranged the meeting—it simply happened by chance. Here's how it unfolded: Our football team, then coached by Nick Saban, was playing Notre Dame in our annual non-conference rivalry game. Tom, an avid football fan who rarely misses a Michigan State University (MSU) football game, decided to drive with his wife, Lupi, to see the game due to the short distance between the two schools. Tom reached out to Nick Saban, who generously provided them with tickets and a parking pass for the game.

Upon arriving at the stadium parking lot, Chief parked next to a gold van that was already there. As he got out of the car, he made eye contact with a gentleman sitting in the van. The man recognized Tom and approached him, asking if he was Tom Izzo. Tom confirmed his identity, and the man then asked if he would like to meet Muhammad Ali.

Tom initially thought the man was joking and started laughing. "Okay, sure. Who do you think you're fooling?" he replied. However, the man insisted that he was serious and explained that Muhammad Ali, accompanied by his wife Lonnie and their son Ahmad, was a big basketball fan who wanted to meet Tom. Tom was skeptical but went over to the van, where the man opened the side doors, revealing Ali and his family. It turned out that the man introducing Tom to Ali was married to Muhammad's personal secretary, who happened to recognize Tom as he parked his car.

In that same year, Tom extended an invitation to Ali and his family to attend our home game against UCONN. Both teams were among the top 10 in the nation at that time. The game was scheduled for an early noon start. Prior to the game, Ali called Tom to inquire about the best time to arrive and spend time together. Tom informed him that the doors would open for spectators two hours before the game. Ali then asked Tom when he would be there, and Tom replied around 9 am. To Tom's surprise, Ali promptly agreed, saying they would arrive at the same time. Tom didn't expect Ali to actually show up at 9 am, but he did, right on schedule.

What an incredible day it turned out to be! It wasn't just because we played well and won the game, but also because Muhammad Ali, *The Greatest*, went above and beyond to make it a truly special day. It all started with his visit to our locker room before the game, where he amazed us with his magic tricks. Among all the impressive things he did, the levitation trick stood out the most.

During the game, there was a huge demand for his autograph and photos. To ensure that everyone had a chance without disturbing those who wanted to watch the game, our building management team set up a dedicated table on the concourse. People could approach him there and get their autographs and pictures taken. It was a thoughtful arrangement that showcased Muhammad Ali's consideration for others.

After the game, Muhammad Ali surprised us once again by revisiting our locker room. He spent more time with our players and staff, further solidifying his incredible character. As if that wasn't enough, he ended the day by joining us as an unexpected guest at our players reunion. It was a testament to his genuine care for people and his unwavering support for our team.

That same season, we went on to win the 2000 national championship. And guess who showed up unannounced as our guest to the championship game? Muhammad Ali, accompanied by a group of approximately ten people. This unexpected arrival caught our ticket staff off guard, and they were initially panicked as they were unprepared to handle such a large group. Fortunately, the staff at Lucas Oil Stadium quickly stepped in and took care of everything for us, ensuring that Muhammad Ali and his companions were well accommodated. I was informed that they arranged a luxury box for him and his guest.

Sometime in late April or early May (I can't recall the exact date), Muhammad and his family generously invited our entire team and staff to his son Ahamad's birthday party in Berrien Springs, Michigan. It's worth noting that Muhammad's residence in Berrien Springs was once the summer home of the infamous gangster Al Capone. Throughout his career, Muhammad acquired the property and converted it into his training camp for his fights. Following his retirement, Muhammad and his wife Lonnie made the decision to permanently reside there, primarily to alleviate the challenges of Muhammad's Parkinson's disease and escape the unwanted attention of celebrity life.

I still remember how excited we all were when we found out we were going to spend the day with Muhammad Ali at his house. Upon our arrival, Ali and his bodyguard were there to greet us as our bus pulled up in front of his place. As everyone got off the bus, Ali shook hands and hugged each person who came with us. I purposely stayed on the bus and watched his interactions with each person because I wanted to witness firsthand the magnitude of his goodness. I also hoped to be the last person, thinking that I might be able to spend a few extra minutes chatting with him. My guess was correct, and I did manage to get those extra minutes.

During our brief conversation, I told him how much my grandfather and I admired him, not only as a boxer but also as a man of tremendous character and great resolve. After expressing my thoughts, he grabbed me by my shirt and pulled me as close to him as he could, whispering in my ear, "But I'm still a N_ _ _ _ _." Then he pushed me back with force, looked me straight in the eye, and smiled.

As we both stood there silence for a brief solitary moment I could feel the depth of his soul and I'm sure he felt mine as he wanted to see if I understood what he meant by what he whispered in my ear. What he didn't know was that I clearly understood it's very meaning long before I ever met him. He than put his arm around me and invited me ride in the golf cart with him up to his house. But I declined because I wanted to actually walk up to the house so I could have a few minutes to process the once in a life time experience I just had with one of, if not the most popular human beings to walk the face of the earth other than Christ.

Not only was the day with Ali an unforgettable experience for myself, but I know for sure it was the same for our players, Chief, and every other person in our group. The experience was so impactful that it is commonly a topic of conversation during many of our yearly team reunions. Overall, it was an unforgettable day filled with Muhammad Ali's incredible presence and his genuine desire to make people's lives better.

Chiefs (HOF) Hall of Fame career is the culmination of a resume filled with a number of firsts, and unfortunately, one of his firsts is entirely overlooked. One that changed the hiring practices of college basketball staffs across the country. Chief had the courage to hire an entire Black assistant coaching staff. Before Chief shocked the college world by hiring three Black assistant coaches, conventional hiring practices were based on race rather than qualification or what was best for the program and its players. Here's what used to happen: if the head coach was either Black or White, the staff had to be racially balanced. In other words, if the head coach was a Black guy, he would only hire one Black assistant, and the other two coaches would be White. On the other hand, if the head coach was a White guy, he would hire one White assistant, and the other two assistants would be Black. However, what was strange about this was that there were still some college basketball staffs that were entirely made up of all-White coaching staffs.

Whereas, on the other hand, you had never seen a staff made up of four Black coaches, let alone three, until Tom Izzo went against the grain and changed the narrative. He changed this racist narrative in the spring of 2007 when I returned to the MSU staff after a short stint at Cleveland State as the head coach and Southern Methodist University as the associate head coach. Tom's decision to bring me back to the staff made Michigan State the first school in college basketball history, outside of the historically black colleges, to have three African assistant coaches on one staff. In my mind, this was something that had been long overdue but was the nature of college basketball under the direction of our country's hypocritical fine college institutions supposedly known for their inclusion, integrity, and equal opportunity.

That year, Tom had several meetings with our staff to discuss how we would be unfairly scrutinized, and that the only way to combat that scrutiny was to win. Sure enough, just as we had discussed, despite winning at a high level, there were people who were constantly trying to fill Tom's ear with the false illusion that THERE WAS SOMETHING MISSING. However, the success of our team during that time in no way suggested that narrative. If you look at the success of our team during those years, you will see that we accomplished everything that you can possibly accomplish outside of winning a national championship. During our brief era as a coaching staff made up of three Black assistant coaches, we were 27-9 overall, finished 4th place in the Big 10, and ended the year with a Sweet Sixteen appearance during our first year together as a staff in the 2007-08 season.

During the following season (2008-09), we had an overall record of 30-7 and secured 1st place in the Big10. We made it to the Final Four and the national championship game, giving us a shot at winning the national championship. However, we lost to North Carolina, the eventual winners, who had a team comprising of 7 NBA first-round draft picks. In our last season together (2009-10), we finished with an overall record of 28-9, once again becoming Big 10 champions. Despite our best player, Kalin Lucas, tearing his Achilles right before halftime in the second game of the tournament, we managed to reach the Final Four. We completely disproved the false narrative that suggested something was missing, which was perpetuated by those individuals who were trying to create that perception. In reality, their concerns had nothing to do with basketball and everything to do with their desire to see coaches of a particular race on the team's bench.

Throughout the pages of this book, I've tried to use basketball analogies as an opportunity to teach valuable life lessons that can improve the quality of life for its readers. The scenario above is one of those opportunities to learn that, despite everything being stacked against you, you can, in the words of the late great Dr. Martin Luther King, overcome. If you're willing to work hard, persevere, and maintain your integrity, no matter the magnitude of your particular circumstances throughout your life's journey.

Tom Izzo is a big-time relationship guy, and I am too, which is why we are probably so close. His ability to forge relationships is why he can let his players come back at him with the same fire and passion that he comes at them. But when they do, they better bring the goods. Many people don't like it from both the perspective of Tom as the coach and the players as well. Then there are those who also view it from a racial perspective, believing that Tom Izzo, a white man, should not aggressively get after his black players openly in public, especially during games that are nationally televised.

There were two incidents in which Tom had encounters with Aaron Henry and Gabe Brown, and these incidents demonstrated exactly that scenario. Some people believe that it is wrong for his black players to aggressively confront their white coach. Unfortunately, those who hold such racial assumptions fail to understand that the confrontations they have witnessed between Tom, the white coach, and his black players can occur without further repercussions from the players, their parents, or the African American community. This is because they all recognize the mutual love, trust, and respect that exists between Tom and his players, which is uncommonly understood by our society as a whole. Such a relationship can only develop as a result of the extra time Tom spends mentoring his players almost daily. Chief and our players have a relationship much like that of family members who often engage in confrontations that most people would consider excessive. However, when confrontations do occur between them, they know that they can maintain their relationships with each other regardless of the magnitude of those confrontations. The outcomes of these confrontations remain healthy because they have given each other permission to aggressively confront one another long before the actual confrontations take place.

To those who have witnessed some of these confrontations between Tom and his players, it would appear that our program is one of the most undisciplined programs in the country. However, contrary to what they might think, ours is one of the most disciplined programs in college basketball when it comes to our players' overall growth and development, both on and off the basketball court. That's because Chief holds our guys accountable in terms of their behavior, academic achievement, and their effort to be great teammates. If you check with anyone who actually knows the inner workings of college basketball programs across the country, they will co-sign the legitimacy of the Michigan State basketball program in terms of discipline.

Chief leaves no stone unturned when it comes to maintaining strong relationships, regardless of the size of someone's role in the success of our program. This is evident through the numerous national championship and Final Four rings and pendants that he personally purchased. He has given these rewards to individuals whom most coaches of his status wouldn't even consider, such as our custodians, Peg and Ray. He doesn't seek recognition for these gestures but rather wants them to know how much he appreciates their contributions to our program's success.

Maya Angelou, the famous poet, captures Tom's unique ability to build, maintain, and strengthen relationships with her quote: "People don't remember what you did; they don't even remember what you said; but they do remember *how you made them feel!"*

OG

Mike Garland

This chapter is supposed to be about me, but it's a challenging task for me because I've always tried to live my life based on the belief in "we" rather than "me." My belief in the collective started from day one of my birth, as I grew up in the home of my grandparents, Dave and Bessie Seed, along with my sister Carol and five other adults. Our residence was a government-subsidized home located in Willow Run, Michigan. It had only two bedrooms, lacking a bathtub or shower, and there was no hot water tank. Our sole source of heat and hot water was a coal stove pipe furnace. If my memory serves me right, the total square footage of the house couldn't have been more than 800 to 900 square feet. The place we lived in consisted of row houses built to accommodate workers who had relocated to Willow Run. The majority of these individuals were from the southern states, who had come to work in the B-29 bomber plant during World War II.

By the time I was born, we were on welfare because my grandfather couldn't work anymore due to a debilitating heart condition, and my grandmother had been diagnosed with terminal cancer. In those days, being on welfare was different from how it is today. Presently, welfare recipients receive what is called a BTE card, allowing them to purchase food in a grocery store discreetly, without anyone knowing they are on welfare. However, when we were on welfare back then, we had to stand in line outside the welfare office and endure public scrutiny to receive government-issued food known as commodities. I still vividly remember what we received because most of the time, I would accompany my grandfather in the line to collect our food. The following list details what the government provided to each family on welfare: canned spam, sardine and hash, a large block of cheese, powdered eggs, powdered milk, a large bag of flour, beans, rice, a large can of lard, and a large can of peanut butter. All the items were packaged in boxes, cans, and bags labeled as U.S. government-issued commodities.

I learned valuable life lessons growing up in a challenging environment where nobody could successfully navigate life without the help of others. When faced with tough times the key to survival was to have a collective mindset. Our living conditions provided me with firsthand experiences of how my family, friends, and neighbors embraced this "we" mentality on a daily basis.

During those days, we resided on a dead-end street called Wall Pole Ct. Out of the ten families on our street, only two owned cars and just one had a phone. Multiple families occupied almost every household due to limited financial means and resources. Sharing a house with another family was necessary because one family alone couldn't make ends meet. We not only shared living spaces but also shared nearly everything else to ensure our survival.

For instance, if someone without a car needed a ride, one of the two car-owning families would willingly offer assistance without expecting anything in return, such as money. They understood that the person in need of a ride likely had nothing to offer them anyway.

However, what was interesting is that most people didn't try to take advantage of the driver but would offer them a small token of appreciation when they have a little (money) something to offer. If they didn't have anything to offer, most people would make it right with the driver the next time they saw them when they did have (money) something to offer.

Another remarkable aspect was that people never tried to inconvenience the drivers who were providing rides. When someone needed a ride, they would often stand on the corner of our street and the main road. Then, as cars approached the stop sign, they would politely ask the driver if they happened to be heading in the direction of their destination. If the driver was, they would receive a ride. If not, the driver would politely decline, and the person in need of a ride would continue to wait until a driver going in their desired direction came along. What was even more impressive was that many times, even when the driver wasn't originally headed toward the person's destination, they would still go out of their way to take them where they needed to go. If the driver was heading to work or had to be somewhere else, he would tell them, "I can drop you off, but you'll need to find a ride back home." This was not a problem because there was always

202

someone heading in the direction of home who would give them a ride.

The Bond's were the only family on our street with a telephone and praise God they were willing to share it with everyone on our street. Whenever someone needed to use the phone they would go to the Bond's house, knock on the door and ask either Mr. or Mrs. Bond if they could use the phone. Usually most people would offer them a dime to use their phone for local calls and I don't know what was offered for long distance. Again just like in the case of getting a ride, if they didn't have the money to give them at the time that they needed to use the phone they would always pay them back when they were able. People always paid up because everyone knew how important it was to help make sure that their phone bill was paid because without the Bonds telephone there would have been no way of making or receiving calls if their phone had got cut off. The Bonds were such gracious people that they also allowed everyone on our street to give out their number to friends and relatives so that they could reach you as well.

Although car rides and use of the phone were the most common things shared they weren't the only things. We all shared food items as well, stuff like bread, milk, coffee, butter, sugar, salt, pepper usually basic staples. The agreement was also the same, if you borrowed something from someone else you just made sure to replace it when you could. Looking back it's without question those experiences during my formative years shaped the belief that I wanted to live a "we" life the rest of my life.

Now, with all of the above that has been said about my upbringing, the underlying question is: Who is Michael Garland? It's both complicated and simple at the same time. That's why I wanted to give you a little bit of my background from my formative years before I try to explain the person that I think I am. In the Bible, when God was asked, "Lord, when we are asked who you are, what do we say?" the Lord said, "Tell them that I AM that I AM." It's a simple answer if you know God, but complicated if you don't. I believe this same thought process applies to who I am and every other person on the face of this earth. That's why it's difficult for me to tell you exactly who I am, if you have preconceived thoughts of me based on the worlds perception of who it's telling you who I AM.

I guess if I were to only identify myself as most people in the world do, then I would have to tell you that I am an accomplished and successful basketball coach. But that explanation makes me small and reduces me to nothing else, which is as far from the truth as the truth itself. I decided many years ago that my life as a basketball coach would be something that I did, as opposed to who I AM. I realized a long time ago that the person I AM has a wide range of interpretations depending on my own perception of myself, not that of other people.

To often what we perceive our success in life to be something that lies in the eyes of its beholder and can only be judged by the many measures of success determined by its beholder. I want you to consider this thought: Can you accurately convey to someone else who you truly are, solely based on your own introspective thoughts, rather than relying on what others have told you about yourself?

This statement raises the question of why I find it impossible to honestly tell you who I AM. While I can share my self-perception, regardless of its accuracy or how others perceive me, it remains subjective.

However, I do believe it is my right to make my own judgment of who I AM and who I AM not. Just like other people have the right to form their own opinions about me. But before I begin to tell you who I believe I AM, let me first clarify who I AM not. I AM not a perfect man without blame, shame, blemishes, regrets and flaws.

I believe I AM simply a man who loves his family, friends, and fellow human beings unconditionally, even though it can be complicated at times. I AM a man who is always ready to lend a helping hand, especially to those in need. I AM a man who finds joy in being a great friend and teammate. I AM a man who genuinely celebrates the success of others without feeling envious or jealous. I am a man with an empathetic heart, someone who willingly gives others my heart, time, resources, and wisdom. A man who lives his life anxious for nothing and at peace with the promises of God. Knowing that when I have done all that I can, that God will take care of the rest. Life has a million success stories; I AM thankful to God that my life is one of them.

POST GAME SPEECH

Epilogue

The writing of this book has been a twelve year journey that has often brought me to tears because often my reflections have taken me back to some of the most joyful times in my life and at other times some of the most painful times in my life. During those moments I've cried both tears of joy and sadness as I attempted to search my inner most being to recover thoughts and memories from my past experiences that could be helpful, interesting and intriguing to the readers of this book. Yet at the same time I wanted to provide readers with pertinent information that could serve as useful tools in their search for answers that are commonly thought of as the secrets to success. Meaningful information that can reshape the minds of readers to think of success as an achievable common place occurrence rather than the aftereffect of hidden secrets.

The book is a little awkward in its presentation because I wanted to make it a multi-faceted collection of effective life changing concepts that pertain to being successful. By using comparative analogies from the game of basketball that can be used as a viable guide to achieving success in the game of life.

AGOGE is a combination of game winning concepts, characteristics and strategies supported by my 7 Intangible Winning Traits of success that are as follows 1) Hard Worker, 2) Self Motivation and Discipline 3)Passion 4) Intensity, Energy & Enthusiasm 5) Leadership 6) Confidence &Competitive Drive and 7) G.U.T.S. I believe these Intangible Winning Traits when appropriately adopted on a daily basis will unlock the door to the simple but yet complicated truths to living a successful life. I decided to name the book AGOGE because it appropriately fits what we've been able to accomplish over the past two decades of championship success. As a result of training our (people) players on the keys that unlock the secrets associated to consistently perform at a *High Performance Maximum Xecution* level for the rest of their lives.

ABOUT THE AUTHOR

"Words can't truly express what Mike Garland mean to me. We've been friends since we met the first night in college and basically have lived the rest of our professional lives together. To say he's just my friend doesn't even scratch the surface of our relationship. He's my brother for life.

"At the same time, we all know that life moves on and this is a great time for Mike to step into a deserved retirement after a tremendous career as a leader in college basketball. The impact he has had on not only this program, but also on nearly every young man he's met while coaching in this sport is incredible. To say that Mike Garland was just a basketball coach would be a disservice. More than anything, Mike has been a teacher and a counselor who has provided life lessons to everyone who came through the doors at the Breslin Center, from players to managers to coaches to staff and definitely to me.

"Mike, his wonderful wife Cynthia and their beautiful family, Simone, Quentin and Michael Ray, have been a big part of our Spartan Family and I thank each of them for what they have done for us.

"If a friend is supposed to have your back, I always knew Mike had mine. Whether in college on the court together, driving his wife to the hospital when she delivered Quentin or just going for all the jogs through campus. Mike will be missed but never forgotten.

"It will be hard for me to come into the office at 7:30 every morning where Mike and I would sit in my office and just talk and not have him there. It will be hard for me to be out of the court or to look down to our bench and not hear his voice or see him there, but Mike Garland's presence at Michigan State is going to be felt for a long, long time."

Made in the USA
Middletown, DE
20 February 2024